The Visionary

The Visionary

Leadership Lessons from RAMESH CHANDRA AGARWAL

Prof. Piyush Kumar Sinha
and
Rupam Singh Gupta

AMARYLLIS

AMARYLLIS

An imprint of Manjul Publishing House Pvt. Ltd.
• C-16, Sector 3, Noida, Uttar Pradesh 201301, India
Website: www.manjulindia.com
Registered Office:
• 2nd Floor, Usha Preet Complex, 42 Malviya Nagar, Bhopal 462 003 – India
Distribution Centres
Ahmedabad, Bengaluru, Chennai, Hyderabad,
Kochi, Kolkata, Mumbai, Noida, Pune

The Visionary - Leadership Lessons from Ramesh Chandra Agarwal
by Prof. Piyush Kumar Sinha and Rupam Singh Gupta

This edition first published in India in 2025

ISBN 978-93-5543-942-0

Printed and bound in India by Replika Press Pvt. Ltd.

Contents

Foreword

Learning is a life-long passion. We accelerate our capabilities by studying the experiences of other leaders. We grow by standing on the shoulders of the great! Let us learn from someone who built the largest Hindi newspaper in India. This entrepreneur has enabled crores of people to know what is happening around the world.

This book draws from the life and legacy of Ramesh Chandra Agarwal, Founder Chairman of the Dainik Bhaskar Group. It serves as a guide for leaders, start-up founders, and management experts. Many first-generation business owners face challenges in building companies that outlast their lifetimes. These challenges include limited succession planning, family conflicts, and an inability to excite the next generation about the business. Ramesh Chandra's legacy stands as a model of sustainable, multi-generational growth. His family has continued to uphold and advance his vision, demonstrating how enduring values and practices can drive success well beyond a founder's lifetime.

The book is structured around three main pillars:

1. **Exhibiting and instilling entrepreneurial spirit into the corporation:** Traditional business schools emphasise managerial and strategic thinking, emphasising the management of scarce resources to accomplish predetermined goals. Ramesh Chandra, however, highlighted entrepreneurial thinking, which makes use of available resources to identify opportunities that are not only unique but also have significant value. Originality and strategic leadership are some of the traits that distinguish entrepreneurial organisations, which exploit the parent company's resources in other enterprises often headed by internal teams, as opposed to corporate venture capital or spinouts. At *Dainik Bhaskar*, Ramesh Chandra created an entrepreneurial culture that avoided bureaucracy, maintained a high tolerance for measured risk, and balanced fresh prospects with judicious resource allocation.

2. **Building focus with a bird's-eye view and a worm's-eye view:** A strategic leader is the one who has the ability to see from both perspectives to get a bigger picture. Ramesh Chandra valued both the broad perspective of a bird's-eye view and the grounded insight of a worm's-eye view. He would often ascend to see the bigger picture while also immersing himself among frontline workers to understand the pulse of the trade and gather timely, relevant insights. This dual approach enhanced his decision-making, allowing him to act swiftly while considering the broader context. As a true visionary leader, he excelled at balancing meticulous planning with ambitious long-term goals.

3. **Navigating the dynamics of family, business and organisation:** It can be difficult for many founders to strike a balance between their personal lives, families, and businesses. Family sacrifices are prevalent because founders are frequently so committed to the company that it takes precedence over other facets of their lives. The founder may become the focal point of important decisions as a result of this devotion, which can also cause a lack of trust and a blurring of the lines between personal and business funds. Ramesh Chandra effectively established an empowered organisation with significant divisions between family and business, as the book explains. With established decision-making procedures, his strategy promoted an organisational culture where staff members felt appreciated and inspired to strive towards the company's goal.

This book offers insights for building enduring family businesses, transferring values across generations, and balancing the often-complex relationships among family, business, and personal life. Through Ramesh Chandra's story, readers learn important lessons about building a robust, entrepreneurial organisation and a sustainable family legacy.

It is a must read. It is captivating!

Please open the book and start the journey.

Dr. Ram Charan

—Advisor to CEOs and Boards of Directors of several prominent companies, and author/co-author of 32 books, including *New York Times* bestselling co-author of *Execution: The Discipline of Getting Things Done.*

Prologue

The car stopped outside the *Dainik Bhaskar* office in Bhopal. Ramesh Chandra Agarwal (Ramesh Chandra) sat inside the car looking at the edifice he had created together with his three sons. He felt different that morning. He was in a pensive mood as he stepped out of his car and walked towards the entrance, taking in the architecture of the place. He remembered the day he bought the land, the day the Agarwal family performed *bhumi poojan*, and the day the foundation of the building was laid. A meeting of the board was set to begin in an hour, where his investors would be discussing the plan he had laid out for the next phase of growth of the DB group.

Ramesh Chandra had built his business on strong fundamentals. *Dainik Bhaskar* had crossed circulation and revenue milestones. The media industry was watching it happen with wide eyes. It wouldn't be audacious to claim that *Dainik Bhaskar* had changed the look and feel of the local language newspapers, and with it their own fortune. People began to regard the newspaper in high esteem, turning to it for authentic and honest take on a story. It soon turned the market trend and in no time became the No. 1 Hindi daily, first in the region and then in the country.

Behind *Dainik Bhaskar's* success lay its founder's clear understanding of where he wanted to go, and why. In his mind, he had a bigger and clearer picture, and a higher purpose for the company. Just like Steve Jobs, he chose to walk a different path other than the usual route taken by others; he chose to 'think differently' so that he could chart a different course for his newspaper, a different but sustainable course focusing on the bigger picture. As a founder, he believed in his vision and he maintained that faith, till his last breath.

The success of any endeavour is often defined by its cause, the reason behind it. Understanding the distinction between the organisation's objective and its leader's responsibility for getting the company to its destination is crucial. Excellent leaders genuinely support and help their subordinates fulfil the objectives of the organisation.

In Ramesh Chandra's case, a bird's-eye view was equally important as a worm's-eye view. To him going to the top – which he did quite frequently and effortlessly – to get an all-around picture was as essential as it was moving among the frontline workers to get the pulse of the trade and first-hand information about what was relevant or what was going on at that point in time. It aided his decision-making, helped him take quick action about things while keeping in mind that everything hinged on it, and helped him make judgements knowing that everything was contextual. He had the ability to recognise what is "good, right, and just for society" while remaining rooted in the specifics of the constantly shifting horizon, just like a genuine visionary leader. He could combine detailed planning with broad goals for the future easily.

Commonly called as practical wisdom, it has its roots in Aristotle's idea of phronesis. It signifies "a true and reasoned state of capacity to act with regard to the things that are good or bad for man", as stated in *Nicomachean Ethics VI.6.* This was wryly interpreted by Samuel Coleridge later as "common sense in an uncommon degree".

Practical wisdom, they believe, is experience-based knowledge that enables people to make morally sound decisions. One can compare it with the Japanese idea of *Toku* – a virtue that inspires people to live their lives in service of the greater good and moral excellence. It is similar to the Indian word, *Yukta*, meaning "suitable". Leaders who, for example, think that the goal of a company, and even the pursuit of profits, is to benefit people and improve society as a whole, adhere to *Yukta* and avoid excess and greed.[1]

'Ramesh Chandra would often say, "Whatever we earn, we should return a portion of it to society. He would never think twice about giving money to a charitable cause, and he never did it so with a hidden agenda,"'

---

[1]*The Wise Leader – How CEOs Can Learn Practical Wisdom to Help Them Do What's Right for Their Companies—and Society,* by Ikujiro Nonaka and Hirotaka Takeuchi, HBR

remembers a former bureaucrat, who looked up to Ramesh Chandra as his mentor.

Managers must comprehend an organization's raison d'être in order to make wise judgements. It is common for businesses to act as though they will do anything to survive, even if it means wreaking havoc on the environment. They would be better served to pursue the common good in order to assure their sustainability. If a company can't provide customers with value, build a future that competitors can't, and uphold the common good, it should not last over the long term.

As one enters the DB head office in Bhopal, one can't miss a huge outline sketch of Mahatma Gandhi and, on the left of the canvas, depiction of his seven social sins. Wealth without work, pleasure without conscience, science without humanity, knowledge without character, politics without principle, commerce without morality, and worship without sacrifice – these sum up Ramesh Chandra's life principles which he followed both in letter and spirit.

In a photograph hanging at the Automotive Hall of Fame in Dearborn, Michigan, Soichiro Honda, the founder of the company is seen at a motorcycle-racing track, crouching down low to put himself at eye level with a rider passing at full speed. Honda has his hands on the ground to feel the vibration and his ears cocked to absorb the sound of the engine. That's how he captured the essence of the motorcycle. "When I look at a motorcycle, I see

> many things," he used to tell his successors. "I see I should do such and such to maneuver past the curve. I think about the next-generation machine. I think, if I do this, it will have more speed. I move naturally into the next process."

Ramesh Chandra believed in a communitarian approach to capitalism, as opposed to the conception of capitalism, which puts business and society against one another. He, like former Toyota president Eiji Toyoda, always said, "One must do what one believes is right and good. Be fearless, act on your convictions, and be who you are." He was an industrialist and a philanthropist who advocated a moral motivation for running a business, and a social purpose in addition to making a profit.

Before making decisions, wise leaders swiftly ascertain the true nature of a problem, project a vision of the future or the likely outcomes, and choose the course of action necessary to realise that vision. They can perceive the essence and intuitively comprehend the nature and significance of things, people, and events.

Experts say, "Grasping the essence requires attention to detail and persistence. If you are going to do something, you must do it relentlessly. Do what is 100% right, concentrate on small things, and continue going back to basics. Unless you do that, you cannot move to the next stage. The secret to success is doing the basics day in and day out."

It's crucial that leaders learn universal truths from

specifics and details. There must be constant interaction between subjective intuition and objective knowledge in order to expand particulars into universals.

> Ratan Tata, the late chairman of the Tata Group, conceived the idea of a $2,500 car in this way. In the now famous story, he noticed an entire family—father, mother, and children—on a scooter, snaking dangerously around cars on a rainy day in Mumbai. He knew that the cheapest car cost five times as much as a scooter did and that families near the bottom of the income pyramid couldn't afford one. Tata realized, right there and then, that those people would buy cars if his company produced them at a price they could afford.

To cultivate the ability to grasp the essence of a problem, intelligent leaders practice three mind-stretching routines. The first is relentlessly asking what the basis of a problem or a situation is. At Toyota, employees ask "Why?" five times to get to the root cause. At Honda, they ask the "A, A0, and A00" questions. *A* questions are about specifications—such as "What should the horsepower of this engine be?" *A0* questions are about concepts—such as "What is the idea behind this engine?" *A00* questions are about the essential goals of the project—such as "What is this engine for?"

Leaders must be able to speak in a language that is accessible to all. They must often employ stories, metaphors, and other figurative language in order to convey a situation's core. This enables people with different backgrounds and diverse experiences to understand concepts intuitively.

Wise leaders like Ramesh Chandra engage in dialogue with as many people as they can, displaying a great level of commitment to communication. Ramesh Chandra used to have discussions, dialogues and debates with his sons, top executives and employees, as well as advisors from varied backgrounds to get a 360-degree view of his vision before taking the plunge. Invariably, before he committed to a project, he always did a recce of that place. He spent days talking to people face-to-face and getting to know the market. He was a people person and knew well that communication is critical to bringing dreams to life. Once he was confident, he simply set the balls rolling.

Effective communicators affect people's hearts and minds, thus rhetoric matters. Knowing others' perspectives and feelings through normal verbal and nonverbal communication helps wise leaders make decisions. Timing is everything as to when to act or when to have a conversation. Consider speeches that have accomplished both goals—Martin Luther King Jr.'s "I have a dream" speech at the Lincoln Memorial in 1963 and Steve Jobs's "Stay hungry, stay foolish" commencement address at Stanford University in 2005. Both had a beginning, middle, and end, were based on personal experience, and repeated the same idea numerous times. King said "I have a dream" eight times and "Let freedom ring" 10 times in the last five minutes of his 17-minute speech. Jobs repeated the phrase "Stay hungry, stay foolish" three times in the last 20 seconds of his 15-minute address.

Ramesh Chandra brought people together and spurred them to act, combining and synthesizing everyone's knowledge and efforts in the single-minded pursuit of his goals. To mobilise people, he utilized all the means suited to the situation. He was stubborn but not shrewd and often created something new and good based on his values of GREATness.

Ground Connection

Result Oriented Outlook

Emotional Association

Analytical Mindset

Trendsetting Capability

1

Going with the Gut

2 December 1984, Bhopal. The City of Lakes witnessed one of the world's worst industrial disasters that killed thousands in one night and scarred the city, which has yet to come to terms with the tragic incident even after three decades. Before the accident took place, there were hopes of attracting investment to the city after Union Carbide, a global company, had set up its factory. But the gas leak happened and left Bhopal and Madhya Pradesh behind in the economic race while the rest of India benefitted from the economic boom. Ramesh Chandra Agarwal was as shaken by that fateful night's tragedy as anyone else in that city. He was in a dilemma though. The media entrepreneur in him saw an opportunity in the tragedy. At the same time, the human in him felt a moral obligation to the people of Bhopal. He set out to tell them the story as it unfolded before his eyes. Team Bhaskar went all out to report the event under the guidance of their torch-bearer leader.

The Bhopal gas tragedy turned out to be a remarkably strategic entrepreneurial opportunity for Ramesh Chandra. His decision to report the tragedy and its aftermath in black and white was a mark of brave and honest journalism that became the foundation on which the newspaper stands today. It was an audacious approach, a turning point in *Dainik Bhaskar*'s growth graph. Nothing, not even heavy political pressure, could deter him from his decision to take the voices of the people to those who mattered and the truth to the common people affected by the gas leak.

> A certain amount of risk-taking is essential. Sometimes you just have to take a chance and correct your mistakes as you go along.

Ramesh Chandra would always listen to his gut and took quick decisions; many such decisions went on to create very successful enterprises. He could sense the pulse of the time. That night, too, he felt that it was the opportune time to turn the crisis to an advantage, which not only benefitted him as an entrepreneur but also established *Dainik Bhaskar* as a name to reckon with in journalism – a newspaper that people looked up to with trust. Ramesh Chandra would not spend too much time on strategising once his mind was set on a project, a striking trait that finds resonance with legendary automaker Lee Iacocca, who believed that "when you don't have all the facts, you sometimes have to draw on your experience. To a certain extent I've always operated by gut feeling. I like to be in the trenches. I was never one of those guys who could just sit around and strategise endlessly. A certain amount of risk-taking is essential. Sometimes you just have to take a chance and correct your mistakes as you go along."

The son of Italian immigrants, Lee Iacocca was introduced to cars first by his father who owned a car rental company and then to retail automobile business at a very young age by one of his friends who owned a car dealership. Iacoccas's father convinced him to go into the automobile business and by the time he was 15, 'his full energy was directed to doing just that'. He credited his father for the marketing instinct in him. Besides owning a car rental firm, his father also owned a couple of movie theatres. Moviegoers would be more excited about special weekend offers than the movie showing in the theatre. Depression changed everything and Iacocca's father lost all his wealth. Lee was six at the time and didn't understand much but was old enough to realise that something very bad had happened. By the time he graduated from college, his mind was set on only one thing – making ten thousand grand a year by the age of 25. Even when he was counted as one among the rich, he would put his money in conservative investments. Iacocca started working at the Ford in August 1946 as a student engineer. In his autobiography, he says "it was the best place in the world to learn how the cars were really made and how the industrial process worked. I was finally seeking the practical application of everything that I had read about in books. I had studied metallurgy, but now I was actually doing it, working at the blast furnaces. I got to run the machinery I had only read about."

In the next 35 years, Iacocca rose through the ranks and became the president of Ford Motor Company. Later, he was toppled in a power play that could have destroyed him. But Iacocca was made of hard mettle, so the shock didn't break him. He joined Chrysler, a sinking ship, and set it to sail. The astute businessman in him revived the dying Chrysler, winning several lost battles and putting it back in gear. He changed the automobile industry in the 1960s, first by creating the phenomenal Ford Mustang and then rebuilding Chrysler, bringing it back from near bankruptcy, to repaying a $1.2 billion government loan so early that Washington didn't know how to cash the cheque.[1]

In just thirty-five years, like Iacocca, Ramesh Chandra had changed the fate of *Dainik Bhaskar*, putting it on

[1]Iacocca Lee and William Novak (1986), *Iacocca: An Autobiography*, Bantam Books.

the national media map. He too started very young. His father first introduced him to the newspaper business, which he later took over and turned into a profitable business. Pawan Agarwal, Ramesh Chandra's youngest son who joined the company during its Jaipur launch in 1996, throws light on what made his father an entrepreneur par excellence and what it took to reach the top: "Ramesh Chandra always focused on fundamental things. For him, in business, one of the core fundamentals was about taking quick decisions. The time taken to arrive at a decision and the time taken to implement it should not be influenced by the past; rather, the past serves as a guide to keep you on the right track. For him, taking decisions quickly meant seizing the moment. He would always say, 'You don't know what's going to happen in the future, say twenty years from now. So seize this moment. If you seize the moment now, it will define what the next twenty to thirty years will be like.'"

Seizing the moment means being agile

Ramesh Chandra was always open to new ideas and did not shy away from embracing them if it appealed to his business sense. He would adopt any idea he felt would propel the company to success. However, he never compromised on his values, which the company follows even today. Change did not unsettle him, even unexpected ones. He navigated them and adapted his ways to them. In doing so, he synergised the change and adaptation initiatives in a successful and sustained manner. He was able to make effective decisions in harmony with these changes and also implemented them in appropriate ways. This learning is fundamental to adaptive responses.

> Ramesh Chandra was always open to new ideas and did not shy away from embracing them if it appealed to his business sense.

Adaptation is more than learning; it requires holistic and culturally relative perspectives. Like several adaptive leaders, Ramesh Chandra would not let his past experiences and limitations block his perceptions of new contexts. What is adaptive is always context-dependent, so a leader must balance what is needed with what can be adapted. Adaptive leaders integrate the processes of assimilation and accommodation to make decisions and chart a route based on information received from different sources. They don't introduce change for the sake of it. They use the information to make decisions that allow them to position their organisation in such a way that it is able to face the challenges of a specific time and space.

> In China, Microsoft was not able to implement its plans to expand successfully. On a suggestion of a Chinese leader, Bill Gates, along with his wife Melinda Gates and another couple friend, set off on a tour of China to get to know the country and its people up close. They toured the country on bikes for a month

to become familiar with the Chinese ways of doing things. The experience benefitted Gates immensely. He re-drafted his strategy for China and made it more inclusive for locals. His new approach was to train locals so that Microsoft could hire them and manage their interests; overlook different values on intellectual property with the longer-term vision of market domination in the Chinese context; and adapt Microsoft to the Chinese ways of doing business for long-term competitiveness. He did not let previous experiences influence his decision-making.[2]

Ramesh Chandra would gather a lot of information before embarking on a project and incorporate them appropriately keeping in mind the interests of all stakeholders. He would always be eager to know more and would not hesitate to interact with younger people or low-level employees in an organisation. What new could he bring to the table was always on his mind. This characteristic pushed him to step into several unchartered territories. He understood that to succeed in today's fast changing and competitive world, companies need to adopt an innovative functional approach. He would create changes if a situation or a project demanded it. That *Dainik Bhaskar* has thrived in a rapidly changing environment proves that it's a stable and dynamic organisation.

[2] Glover Jerry, Gordon Jones, and Harris Friedman (2002), '*Adaptive Leadership: When Change Is Not Enough*', in *The Organization Development Journal*, Summer 2002, Volume 20, Number 2, pp. 15–31.

Ramesh Chandra would always focus on the readers. He readily adjusted to environmental changes as he was open and inclusive. That's why the organisation has evolved continually tackling challenges along the way under the agile leadership of its founder. Adapting does not always require changes. In some cases, adaptation involves finding ways of using the past to get to the future. Agile leaders can adapt to an ever-changing and uncertain environment. They set out to be continuous learners and have a growth mindset, always looking for ways to improve products, services and themselves.[3]

Inspired partly by the success of the *USA Today*, *Dainik Bhaskar*, based out of Madhya Pradesh, made strategic entries in several markets in western and northern India in the early 1990s and claimed leading positions from the first day of their entry in most of these markets. Even formidable competitors were overwhelmed by the daily's trailblazing ways. *Dainik Bhaskar* created its circulation by adding newer segments in the paper and duplicating readership in their target households. The result was an increase in overall market circulation, though a drop in readership ratio. His eldest son, Sudhir Agarwal, who was the first to join his father's business, believes that the aggressive entry gave *Dainik Bhaskar* an unprecedented debut in most of its markets. However, it is the newspaper's content that has kept readers loyal

[3]Rigby, Darrell K., Jeff Sutherland, and Hirotaka Takeuchi, '*Embracing Agile: How to Master the Process That's Transforming Management: Experimentation*'; *Harvard Business Review*. https://hbr. org/2016/05/ embracing-agile (2016).

to them over the years. The success story that started from Jaipur in 1996, where it overwhelmed the reigning leadership of *Rajasthan Patrika*, encouraged them to enter other parts of the state and emerge as the largest daily in Rajasthan.[4]

Being agile also means being innovative. Agile organisations tend to have a 70 per cent chance of being in the top quartile of organisational health, the best indicator of long-term performance. Such companies also achieve 'greater customer centricity, faster time to market, higher revenue growth, lower costs, and a more engaged workforce'.[5] Ramesh Chandra built an agile organisation based on a *shared purpose and vision* that acted as a guide with a focus on creating value for stakeholders with flexibility to quickly *sense and seize opportunities*. He has also created a dense network of empowered teams that operate with high standards of alignment, accountability, expertise, transparency, and collaboration. The rapid cycles of thinking and doing were closely aligned to their process of creativity and accomplishment. He could engage and empower everyone in the organisation. Team Bhaskar could create value quickly, collaboratively, and effectively and act in team-oriented ways and become involved in making the strategic and organisational decisions that would affect them and their work.

---

[4]Sinha, Piyush Kumar and Kunjesh Pariher (2002), *Dainik Bhaskar*, *Asian Case Research Journal*, Vol. 6, Issue 2, pp. 167–204.

[5]Wouter Aghina, Karin Ahlback, Aaron De Smet, Gerald Lackey, Michael Lurie, Monica Murarka, and Christopher Handscomb (2018), *The Five Trademarks of Agile Organizations*, McKinsey Report, 2018.

Using Gut

Is it okay to make decisions based on one's gut feelings? Should leaders rely on their intuition to make important choices? Research shows that they should consider two things before deciding whether to trust their gut. First, identify the problem. Second, weigh all options and their levels of 'unknowability'. Leaders use their intuition when all calculations of probabilities and risks appear unrealistic and unfeasible. When a company plans to launch a new product, it conducts surveys to study the market, potential customers and competitors. In case the company, despite the analysis, is not sure, an agile leader listens to instinct and makes a decision.[6] One can't disregard the power of human intuition. Many leaders have more faith in it than data or analysis to run their businesses. But intuitive decisions can be unreliable in the absence of analysis. If it can lead to success, then it can also lead to failures. So, what should leaders do when faced with too many choices in too little time? The answer lies in the use of new decision support tools that mobilise the power of human intuition. These tools amplify not only the mind's analytical power but also its creative potential.[7]

The newspaper man, Ramesh Chandra, always trusted his gut and used his intuition to make decisions. This helped speed up his decision-making timetables. At the same time,

---

[6]Laura Huang, *When It's OK to Trust Your Gut On a Big Decision*, HBR.ORG, 22 October 2019.

[7]Bonabeau, Eric. 'Don't Trust Your Gut'. Harvard Business Review, 81.5 (2003): pp. 116–23.

he would also analyse lot of information. According to Sudhir, he was intuitive but also had the innate ability to see and gather information that others may miss.

"When we went to Rajasthan for the Jaipur launch," recollects Ramesh Chandra's eldest son, "we all saw a saturated market totally dominated by *Patrika*, which had moved from 60 per cent to 90 per cent market share in the past five years. It had handled national competitors *Nav Bharat Times* and *The Times of India*. The trade and the readers were super loyal to them; they read only *Patrika*. That is how we all defined the market. That is how everybody else in the country defined it. That was common knowledge. But Ramesh Chandra approached it very differently."

> "When my brothers and I told him that ninety per cent of the market is dominated by this newspaper, he asked us, 'What does dominance mean?'"
>
> "Dominance means that a market is controlled by a single company like Facebook or Google," we said.
>
> "What market?" he retorted.
>
> "It's a newspaper market," we said.
>
> "Who constitutes a newspaper market?" he asked.
>
> "A newspaper market is constituted by readers."
>
> "What about people who don't read?" he asked.
>
> "People who don't read are illiterate," was our response.
>
> "Really?" he exclaimed.
>
> "Yes."
>
> "OK, let's look it up," he said.
>
> "'So, we dug up the data – census, readership,

population, reviews. Ramesh Chandra then asked us to prepare a list of (a) number of people living in brick-and-mortar houses, (b) number of literate people, and (c) number of people with a gas and electricity connection. According to him, a person with a gas and electricity connection and a voter's ID could be classified as part of the population that can read. Whether the person read a newspaper or not was secondary. What was important was that they could read. It was data for Ramesh Chandra. Then he asked us to find out what these so-called illiterate people did. He concluded that this market was characterised by only 27 per cent literacy, and among those who could read, only a fraction actually read any newspaper. By challenging the prevailing theory that a particular newspaper dominated the market, he turned it upside down. Analysing the available data, he reached a compelling conclusion: this market remained largely untapped, as 73 per cent of the population did not read any newspapers at all."'

Intuition and rationality: Two sides of the same coin

The intelligence of non-conscious thought and when it should be used is gaining ground as the pressure to make quick decisions in a limited time span is increasing.[8] So is the potential of intuition. Research suggests that

[8]Hofmann, Wilheim, and Timothy D. Wilson. *Consciousness, Introspection, and the Adaptive Unconscious.* (2010).

decomposable tasks, for example, mathematical solutions, which can be attempted by breaking them into small tasks use analytical decision-making whereas non-decomposable tasks are more suited to intuitive thinking. However, the effectiveness of intuition is ensured only when one has attained expertise in the focal domain – the greater one's domain expertise, the more effective will be their intuitive thinking.

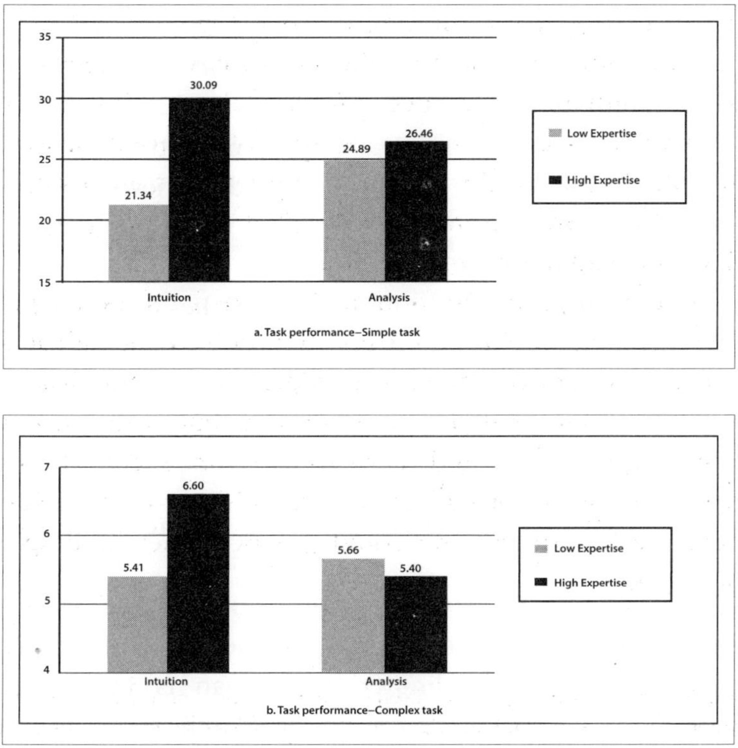

Figure 1.1 – Usage of intuition and analysis in performing different tasks.

Intuition and rationality are two sides of the same coin. Intuitive thinking is automatic, a hunch based on emotion and feeling, something that is holistic and non-verbal. Conscious thinking is rational, analytical, to an extent emotion-free and verbal. Expertise and feeling, the two aspects of intuition, are interlinked and develop below the level of conscious awareness. Intentional or rational thinking originates in the conscious awareness beside the intuitive system. It's not that the two cannot be bridged. The challenge lies in linking the two together and using intuition with rationality to make use of intuitive judgements. Adam Smith has said successful are those who 'do not necessarily have a complete portrait of themselves, warts and all, but they do have the ability to stop abruptly when their own intuition and what is happening out there are suddenly out of kilter'.[9]

Studies support the notion that when the going gets tough, leaders go with their gut, but with the qualification that they do not overthink their decisions.[10] Some leaders are of the view that data is important but while dealing with people one should learn to trust one's gut. Though there's no magic formula to achieve 100 per cent success, there are few things one could practice when wading in the unknown.

---

[9]Sadler-Smith, Eugene, and Erella Shefy. 'The intuitive executive: Understanding and Applying "gut feel" in decision-making.' Academy of Management Perspectives, 18.4 (2004): pp. 76–91.

[10]Mikels, Joseph A., et al. 'Should I go with my gut? Investigating the benefits of emotion-focused decision making.' *Emotion*, 11.4 (2011): p. 743.

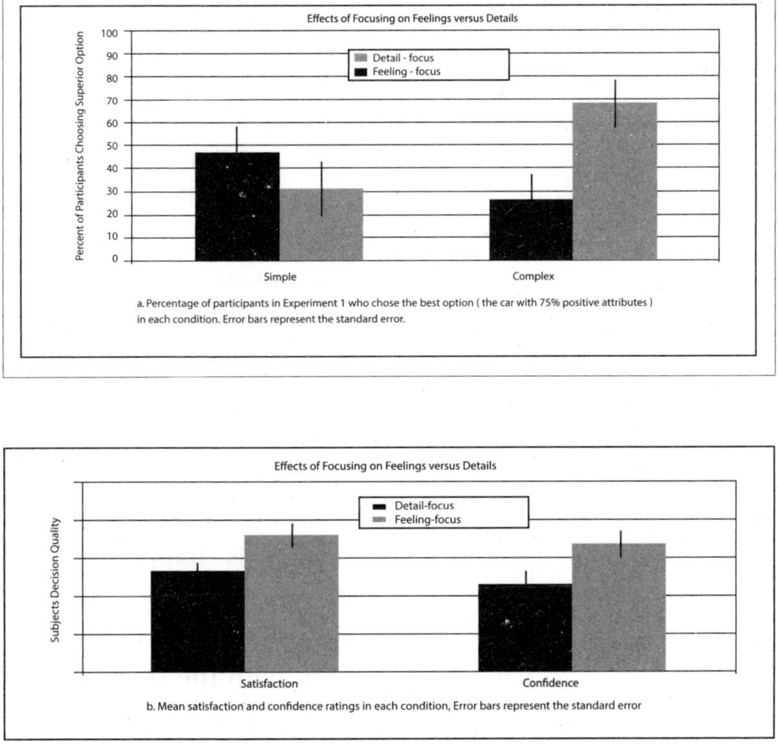

a. Percentage of participants in Experiment 1 who chose the best option (the car with 75% positive attributes) in each condition. Error bars represent the standard error.

b. Mean satisfaction and confidence ratings in each condition, Error bars represent the standard error

Figure 1.2 – Effects of focusing on feelings versus details

Lucidchart co-founder and CEO Karl Sun cultivates a culture of experimentation. 'I give my teams the ability to try things. Sometimes they'll want to experiment with ideas that go against every fibre of your being but those often turn out to be the biggest wins. One of the engineers at Lucid came up with a crazy idea to build a flowchart explaining the popular Internet meme around "doggos". It didn't go with Lucid tradition but the creative team went ahead with it and made a video. The CMO gave its nod to publish it and to everyone's surprise, the video became viral. It garnered 33 million views, 400K comments and shares, and 850K likes till 26 June 2018. The team created several flowcharts around other Internet memes and they all went viral. The campaign increased YouTube watch time by 600 per cent and 20x the number of YouTube subscribers. The videos are inexpensive to create and easy to get out there, and they are introducing the idea of diagramming to people who were nowhere near that universe.'

For Karl it is easy to go full force with data that seem so accurate. But cautions against blindly trusting as 'numbers aren't always perfect and don't tell the complete story'. An external analysis on customer base, which he thought was good for the company, on further review, turned out to be wrong. It meant he had to do a 180-degree pivot and go for another course that went against his gut. It was a tough call but it was better to course-correct then and there. So, examine the data, but don't let it rule one's move.

Initially, one may not be too sure of one's gut feeling and hesitate in using it in decision making. But, as one grows and gains experience, one becomes wiser and more confident. Karl Sun experienced it and found it true in the hiring process. After conducting multiple interviews and meeting candidates, he could confidently rely on his gut. Many a time, candidates who don't seem they would be successful on paper, turn out to be nearly always the right choice for the job. According to him, trusting one's gut can be nerve-wracking at times, but remember that practice makes perfect.[11]

Ramesh Chandra was very thorough with his groundwork and always gathered the minutest details before embarking on a new project. The Jaipur launch was a milestone in the group's growth graph as it was their first foray into a new state. So he worked on all the details till he was satisfied. His next question for his sons was what would inspire the 73 per cent non-readers to read a newspaper. "They lose interest the moment they hear the word *newspaper*. So, go to the heart of the newspaper and look at its functions. What can it do to somebody's life? How it can influence a housewife, an office-goer or a student? What do they want to read in a newspaper?" He urged his team to find out everything that mattered to a reader.

His words, "let's go and find out" were like a magic charm that motivated everyone who worked with him. Never before had a newspaper asked its readers what they wanted to read. So, the team set out to find out

[11]https://www.saastr.com/top-lessons-learned-lucidchart-karl-sun/accessed on 27-07-2022.

what the readers wanted. For the first time, the intuitive Ramesh Chandra Agarwal took a practical approach, "Go to every house of this 73 per cent and talk to them. We won't tell them that we are a newspaper. Ask them why they don't read a newspaper and what will make them read one," he asked the team. He would never instruct. He would say, "*Apan aisa karte hain* [let's do it this way]". The team culled out ten to fifteen broad points from the list of things people wanted to read. Ramesh Chandra then asked the team to go back to the same people and tell them about the points that would be served in their newspaper. "Just as it's difficult to offer 20 different cuisines to cater to everyone's individual preferences during dinner, we can't cover everything in a newspaper," he justified.

Dainik Bhaskar's Jaipur edition was launched on 19 December 1996. Everything else, as they say, is history.

An intuitive decision maker's mind

Should one listen to one's head (analytical/cognitive), or follow the heart (emotional/affective) or go by gut (intuition) in decision-making? All of us have three 'brains' involved in decision making – the first one in our head, the second in our heart, and the third in our gut (stomach).[12] Since no two individuals are alike, differences

[12]Soosalu, Grant, Suzanne Henwood, and Arun Deo. 'Head, heart, and gut in decision making: development of a multiple brain preference questionnaire.' *SAGE Open* 9.1 (2019): 2158244019837439.

in competencies and preferences are bound to happen when it comes to decision-making. Over time, emotions (heart) and instincts/feelings (gut) evolve and so do the nervous system, the cardiac network and the head-brain.[13] Different people use head, heart, and gut differently as per their preferences in decision making.[14]

Ramesh Chandra seldom went by data (head), hearsay (heart) or ground reality (head + heart) alone. He combined all the three. Ideas he heard from the people kept him going; then he would collect necessary data and check the ground reality, and then again go back to the people to check the truth, and then combine the three. He never relied on just one of these. It usually happens that most of the entrepreneurs get carried away by one of these. They make decisions either by data, by what people say or by the ground reality. Ramesh Chandra always combined all these three and kept moving quickly because these three can also slow one down. Of course, instinct would kick in first and propel him to go to people to find out what they wanted.

Head, heart and gut are used together by leaders in complex business environments, leading to more effective decisions. Complex times require complete leaders, those capable of using their head, their heart, and their guts

---

[13]Haselton, M., and Ketelaar, T. (2006). Irrational emotions or emotional wisdom? In J. P. Forgas (Ed.), *Affect in social thinking and behavior* (pp. 21–39). New York, NY: Psychology Press.

[14]Bishopric, N. (2005). *Evolution of the heart from bacteria to man. Annals of the New York Academy of Sciences*, 1047, pp. 13–29.

as situations demand.[15] In adaptive leadership, 'solutions to technical problems lie in the head and solving them requires intellect and logic. Solutions to adaptive problems lie in the stomach and the heart and rely on changing people's beliefs, habits, ways of working or ways of life'.[16]

Head Brain Prime Functions

Cognitive perception—cognition, perception, pattern recognition

Thinking—reasoning, abstraction, analysis, synthesis, metacognition

Making meaning—semantic processing, language, narrative, metaphor

Heart Brain Prime Functions

Emoting—emotional processing (e.g., anger, grief, hatred, joy, happiness)

Values—processing what's important and their priorities

Relational affect—feelings of love/hate/indifference, compassion/ uncaring, like/dislike

---

[15]Dotlich, D., Cairo, P., and Rhinesmith, S. (2006). *Head, heart & guts – How the world's best companies develop complete leaders*. Hoboken, NJ: John Wiley.
[16]Heifetz, R., and Linsky, M. (2004). 'When leadership spells danger'. *Educational Leadership*, 61 (7), pp. 33–38.

Gut Brain Prime Functions

Core identity—a deep and visceral sense of core self, and determining at the deepest levels what is 'self' versus 'not-self'

Self-preservation—protection of self, safety, boundaries, hungers and aversions

Mobilization—motility, impulse for action, gutsy courage and the will to act[17]

If Jaipur was *Danik Bhaskar*'s first step outside Madhya Pradesh, it was also the biggest risk the group had taken so far to gain a foothold in a new territory. Ramesh Chandra's fearlessness to take the new market by storm came from his gut feeling to keep moving ahead. It's the reason he invested whatever he had in reserve. Pawan remembers his businessman father's resolute mind when he saw him from close quarters for the first time. That was about commitment. He had an intuition that it's a big market, it's a big opportunity. The company would get into trouble if it wasn't successful. Ramesh Chandra said, "That's the reason a lot of people would not want to do it. But it's a big opportunity and we can take that risk. I have to make it work now that I have taken the risk", he said. He made it work with his high level of commitment.

[17]Soosalu, G., and Oka, M. (2012). *m*BIT and leadership. Retrieved from http://www.mbraining.com/mbit-and-leadership.

Ramesh Chandra's ability to go with his instinct would often reap benefits. Entering Chandigarh, considered till then a predominantly English market, was one such intuitive decision that went on to become a big success, breaking the myth of English readership and creating a new lingo for Hindi readership. Before he went to Chandigarh, nobody thought it could be a Hindi market. When he went to the market and talked to people, he realised that they knew Hindi very well. He thought if he gave a top-class product, it would draw its own readership. So, he went with the market and the people. He found that the people in Chandigarh did not know typical Hindi words. *Bhaskar* became the first Hindi newspaper to experiment with language and introduce some commonly used Hindi words to replace several tongue-twister words. So *vidyut* became *bijli*, *vishwavidyalaya* became college/university, *zila magistrate* became collector. Thus, it gave birth to a new vocabulary, an actual dictionary. "We didn't destroy the language but didn't use typical Hindi words either, because during day-to-day conversation people do not use these words. Even people in villages are not using such words. Nobody says *main vidyut office ja raha hoon*. They say *main bijli office ja raha hoon,'* says Sudhir. Chandigarh marked a distinct shift in *Dainik Bhaskar*'s character – entry into an English domain and the introduction of colloquial words that are easy to understand. The practice became commonplace. Not only did other editions of the Dainik Bhaskar adopt this practice, but many other newspapers also followed suit.

Charting unknown territories

Ramesh Chandra would always be on the move exploring unknown territories and testing new waters. Once he established *Dainik Bhaskar* as a successful brand, he began spreading his wings in different sectors like realty, oil and textile. Wading in unknown waters meant thinking on one's feet. This never deterred him from reflecting on his previous experiences, whether they were successful or not. In fact, the adventure would spur his desire to keep moving ahead and expanding his territory. [18]

He was inquisitive and would ask a lot of questions before investing in a venture. Was the business viable? What was the government policy? What were the risks involved? He would elicit all the necessary information to make decisions about opportunities that he had not seen before with 'innovative, disruptive technologies that may challenge existing ways of thinking'.

For agile leaders, formal analysis does not undermine intuitions. So far as risks were concerned, Ramesh Chandra never discounted formal analyses nor did he disregard his gut feeling. He believed in his experience-based intuitive assessments of an enterprise. In contrast to the choice under risk, ambiguity and uncertainty require attention be paid to the belief formation process, including the choice of appropriate models and theories that can be used to

---

[18]Huang, Laura, and Jone L. Pearce. 'Managing the unknowable: The effectiveness of early-stage investor gut feel in entrepreneurial investment decisions.' *Administrative Science Quarterly* 60.4 (2015): pp. 634–670.

guide action.[19] When faced with risks, keeping in mind the successes he had had previously, Ramesh Chandra relied on intuition to identify opportunities that he could build into extraordinarily successful companies. He would always converse with his sons, friends, people in the know, and anyone who could give him important inputs about a project he was keen to invest in. Of course, his decisions would be guided by his hunch. As Heath and Tversky would say, he had complete confidence in his own expert judgements.[20]

[19]Kleindorfer, P. R. (2010). 'Reflections on decision-making under uncertainty' In F. X. Diebold, N. A. Doherty, and R. J. Herring (eds.), *The Known, the Unknown, and the Unknowable in Financial Risk Management*: pp. 194–209. Princeton, NJ: Princeton University Press.

[20] Heath, C., and A. Tversky (1991). 'Preference and belief: Ambiguity and competence in choice.' Journal of Risk and Uncertainty, 4: pp. 5–28.

2

An Ear to the Ground

3 April 1997. Ajmer, Rajasthan. *Dainik Bhaskar* launched its third edition in the city, just three months after successfully launching the newspaper in Jaipur. Everyone was surprised – how was Ramesh Chandra able to launch in a second city in such a short span of time? His decision had, in fact, surprised his sons too, who had at first dismissed his plan as they were preoccupied with the Jaipur edition, which was not even a month old. But Ramesh Chandra was insistent. He had already visited Ajmer around mid-January and sensed an opportunity, a potential market for his newspaper. He had walked the streets of the city to get a feel of the place and talked to the locals to know their likes and dislikes, their preferences and other mundane things they did every day.

He found that *Navjyoti* was the only daily catering to the Ajmer readership. Somehow despite capturing the entire Rajasthan newspaper market, *Patrika* had not been able to break *Navjyoti*'s monopoly in Ajmer. Sudhir remembers the spark in his father's eyes when he said, "Let's do it before *Patrika* or anyone else smells the opportunity". There was no time for surveys. Ramesh Chandra had already gathered basic data and had assessed the ground reality. All they needed was a building and other support to set up a press to start the edition. Inspired by his father's speedy decision, Sudhir too got into the act. He dashed off to Ajmer to put things in order. Within a week the location for the building was finalised, the office was set up and the people, handpicked from other editions, were ready to start work.

To an outsider, the entire sequence of events leading up to the launch would seem like a movie running in fast-forward motion. In reality, it was done meticulously, leaving no room for a mishap. *Danik Bhaskar* took the pole position in Ajmer from the first day itself, just like its Jaipur edition.

Identifying opportunity

What worked for Ramesh Chandra often does not work for others. First and foremost, he was self-aware and understood his surroundings. Within that context, he gave shape to opportunities. When he moved around Ajmer talking to its people, he looked for what's missing and identified the gaps in the market. He made his calculations based on the details collected first-hand and began working on his idea. Linking information derived from various sources formed the basis of the business opportunity. Second, he applied both intuitive and analytical processes to approach his idea. Drawing on his past experiences, his instinct helped him recognise an opportunity, whereas the rational mind generated data that would guide his next steps. In this way, he used one process to inform another to move forward. Third, Ramesh Chandra was able to factor in social and economic responsibility and focus on customer benefits without compromising on the quality of news reports.[21]

Entrepreneurs tend to have prior information necessary to identify an opportunity and cognitive properties necessary to value it.[22] Broadly, opportunity is a chance one perceives and then develops to deliver better quality products or services to the market by combining different resources. An entrepreneur works on an opportunity from its elemental form and creates a business plan. Entrepreneurial decisions are creative decisions. That is, the entrepreneur constructs the means, the ends or both. It is not about whether there is optimal use of resources. It is about what customers want, what resources the entrepreneurs can assemble and what kind of products these resources can produce. 'It is the successful identification of relevant ends and means (rather than the efficient utilisation of means

[21]Wilson, H. J., D. Greenberg, and K. McKone-Sweet. 'How entrepreneurs find opportunity.' *Harvard Business Review* Blog Network. http://blogs.hbr. org/cs/2011/09/*entrepreneurs_find_opportunity*. html (2011).

[22]Shane, S. & Venkataraman, S. 2000. The promise of entrepreneurship as a field of research. Academy of Management Review 25, pp. 217–226.

to achieve ends) which makes the "right" decision on product quality.'[23] [24]

Ramesh Chandra would chance upon an idea and float it to his team responsible for that business. *"I think it has potential and we must do it,"* would often be his opening statement during such meetings. They would discuss, argue and then reach a common ground to build on that idea. During the initial days after the Jaipur launch, Sudhir remembers his father waiting for him at 8.30 a.m. one day. In those days, Sudhir and his brothers would reach home around 4.00 a.m. after the newspaper for that day had been dispatched. Ramesh Chandra wanted to discuss the Ajmer project. It was too early in the morning for Sudhir to have a serious discussion, but in Ramesh Chandra's mind the matter needed their immediate attention. Girish and Pawan were also asked to join them. They worked on the idea and identified problems it might throw at them. Ramesh Chandra showed them how he could 'fit' his product between the needs of that market and resources they had.

Entrepreneurs work with two types of opportunities – codified and tacit. A codified opportunity presents a structured or well-defined situation wherein an entrepreneur wants to take advantage of the market inefficiency in a less-than-saturated market.[25] Ajmer, for instance, was a codified

---

[23]Eckhardt, J. and Shane, S. (2003) 'Opportunities and Entrepreneurship', *Journal of Management* 29: pp. 333–49.

[24]Kirzner, Israel M. 1973. *Competition and Entrepreneurship.* Chicago: University of Chicago Press.

[25]It should be noted that the distinction between codified and tacit

opportunity for Ramesh Chandra. It didn't require much improvement in the product. The group worked on the gap in the market and started the edition using the resources they had. A tacit opportunity, on the other hand, allows more scope for improvements or innovations because of its inarticulable nature. Most of Ramesh Chandra's projects could be termed as tacit opportunities, including the launch of Radio FM.

Akio Morita, co-founder of Sony Corporation of America, was an expert at finding a gap and filling it. He moved to America in 1963 with his family to expand his business because he saw potential in the market. He said if he had to sell his products to Americans, he needed to know them and how they lived. He began to socialise and throw parties to build a solid network of contacts. He noticed Americans' love for music. They would listen to it in their cars and even carried large stereos to the beach and park. This gave him an idea to create a

---

opportunities represent two anchor points on a continuum rather than a dichotomy. Rather than existing as mutually exclusive categories, these two forms of opportunities—codified and tacit—exist along a continuum ranging from a low to a high degree of tacitness (for a similar argument of the nature of knowledge, see Ambrosini, Veronique, and Cliff Bowman. 'Tacit knowledge: Some suggestions for operationalization'. *Journal of Management Studies* 38.6 (2001): pp. 811–829.

Tacit opportunities are likely to become more codified through the passage of time. The more codified the opportunity becomes, the lower the entrepreneurial rents that are likely to be gained through the exploitation of the opportunity (ibid 3).

product that was portable with high-quality sound, something that allowed a person to listen to music while doing something else. Thus, Walkman was born, one of Sony's most popular and profitable products.

The Walkman proved a huge success for Sony because of its technology. No other company could produce anything like it as its technology was difficult to copy. So, it was over two years before other competing models were launched in the market. Sony had by then sold 20 million units, leading the company to gain worldwide recognition. Morita was the man responsible for making 'Made in Japan' synonymous with several firsts in the development of new electronics product.[26]

Opportunities are evaluated at different stages of their development. When *Dainik Bhaskar* planned to enter Jaipur, investigations were made into what the market needed. A household survey was launched to find out the reading habits of those who subscribed to newspapers. Those who were literate but did not read any newspaper or magazine were also approached to know what they would want to read in a newspaper. It was a first-of-its-kind survey to know people's preferences. The Bhaskar team pursued the research till it required no further consideration. They then went back to the people with a

[26]Akio Morita, Edwin Reingold, Mitsuko Shimomura, *Made in Japan*, published in 1986 by Robert Laffont.

draft newspaper and showed them what kind of stories the new daily planned to deliver. It also kept the price of the daily lower than the leading newspaper at that time. Once resources were committed based on their evaluation of the survey, a plan was set into motion that translated into huge economic success.

Entrepreneurs pass opportunities through a stage-gate process and evaluate them on factors like returns, risks, resources (financial and otherwise), responsibilities and goals.[27] Some entrepreneurs may discard a chance based on these indicators, while another may go for it. One of Ramesh Chandra's friends advised him to enter into the liquor business as it had good prospects. Ramesh Chandra didn't have much idea about the trade. He procured the required licence from the government and started the business. Sudhir was assigned to oversee it. Very soon they realised that the business required large cash dealings. After a couple of months into it, Sudhir began to have qualms about continuing it. He approached his father with his misgivings. Ramesh Chandra, who by then had a fair idea what the trade entailed, decided to sell it at once. He was uneasy about the nature of the business as it went against his values. They sold it off the very next day even though they incurred a huge loss. The number of businesses that see the light of day is less as compared to market needs or resources perceived. Any

[27]Grönlund, Johan, David Rönnberg Sjödin, and Johan Frishammar. 'Open innovation and the stage-gate process: A revised model for new product development'. *California management review* 52.3 (2010): pp. 106–131.

opportunity that does not pass through a 'gate' must be revised or even terminated. In this case, Ramesh Chandra shelved the opportunity. He created twelve businesses; seven of them have flourished.

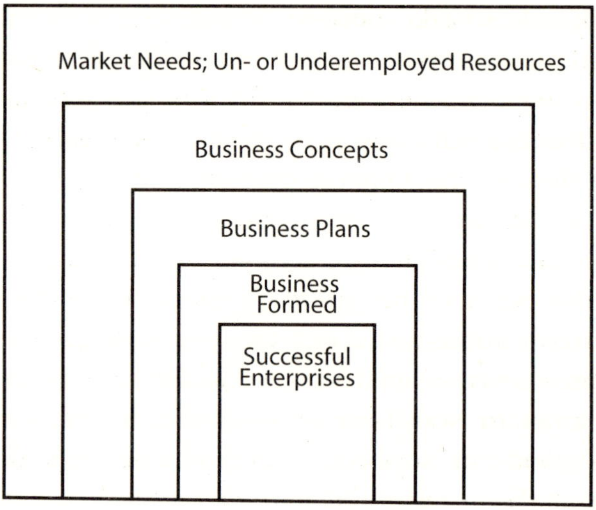

Figure 2.1 – From a market need to a successful enterprise: the Stage Gate Process[28]

Entrepreneurial alertness

Entrepreneurs need to be alert to sense an opportunity others may have missed. The Bhaskar Group forayed into the realty sector by building a shopping mall in Bhopal.

---

[28]Ardichvili, Alexander, Richard Cardozo, and Sourav Ray. 'A theory of entrepreneurial opportunity identification and development'. Journal of Business venturing 18.1 (2003): 105-123.

The city did not have a mall until then. The Bhaskar Group could have built a run-of-the-mill mall, as it would be the first mall in a tier-II city. But Ramesh Chandra wanted the people of Bhopal to get a metro-like shopping experience. Thanks to his entrepreneurial awareness,[29] he was able to take note of behavioural patterns in the market and unmet needs and interests of the consumers. So, DB City came up in the heart of Bhopal in August 2010. Ramesh Chandra had a knack for putting himself in the flow of information that increased his chances of encountering an opportunity. Like any experienced and successful entrepreneur, he would then focus his energy on risks because he could perceive reality and infer likely implications and consequences. Veridical perception and interpretation enabled him to detect any change in the market or social world that may not be conducive to his goods or services. His alertness allowed him to ascertain the commercial potential of any situation. An individual's knowledge and beliefs about how physical and social worlds work depend on his mental models or schemas that help direct his attention and guide information processing and reasoning for any specific event, real or imagined.[30]

---

[29]Ray, Sourav, and Richard Cardozo. "Sensitivity and creativity in entrepreneurial opportunity recognition: a framework for empirical investigation." Sixth Global Entrepreneurship Research Conference, Imperial College, London. 1996.

[30]Kaish, Stanley, and Benjamin Gilad. 'Characteristics of opportunities search of entrepreneurs versus executives: Sources, interests, general alertness'. *Journal of Business Venturing* 6.1 (1991): pp. 45-61.

Ramesh Chandra had more accurate mental models. Adversity did not scare him, because he knew that ups and downs are two sides of the same coin. A crisis never bothered him. He would say, "OK, this has happened, let's see it through". Ramesh Chandra once entered the edible oil business. He invested a couple of crores of rupees in a plant in Sri Lanka. The plant was to make palm oil, which would be shipped to India. He had one refinery in Madhya Pradesh and another one in Maharashtra near a port. The plan was to refine oil and sell it in the local market as well as export it. Construction at the refinery site had begun when the central government changed policies and levied duty on imports. The business became unviable as the cost shot up significantly. Ramesh Chandra, however, wasn't perturbed as to what would become of the Rs 1,800 crore plant in Maharashtra. He said, "Fine, this won't work out, so let's think of something else'. He moved on. Nothing stopped him.

Experts have more complex schema that crosslinks to other schemas. It allows them to see patterns and detect anomalies more quickly. For Ramesh Chandra, this schema would activate habitually alerting him to even ambiguous situations. Therefore, guiding his perceptions and understanding to the extent that he was able to notice without search a gap or irregularity.

Ramesh Chandra's second son Girish, who manages the marketing and sales of the media business, says that though his father's circle of friends was very limited, all the knowledge about various projects that he had was based on his interactions with people he met along the way – he would interact with anybody, generate ideas based on his conversations, and work on that. He was able to visualise things and never doubted who would do execute an idea or how it would be done. Being adaptable and flexible were his biggest assets, so he could always respond quickly to changes and strategise accordingly. Once he had an idea, he would put together a team and get the ball rolling. He was always ready to face setbacks if the team did not perform well and the business suffered. In the 90s, the group owned a small cement plant near Indore. Girish remembers visiting it once in his lifetime. His father was not an expert in that business. The team he had created to run it couldn't live up to his expectations. Eventually, the business failed and the plant had to be sold off. But like a man with a purpose, he kept moving without lingering on his failures.

Alertness directs attention towards the novel, unusual or contrary and guides information processing towards the integration of the unusual event even if it means rethinking the existing means–ends framework or the way things are done. Most market actors accept information as given, but alert individuals look for some change. The near-expert status, brought on by habitual use, allows the alert individual to detect a pattern amid the noise that any change would generate. The likelihood of extensive cross-linkages to industry schema and socio-political schema enabled the alert individuals to consider the implications of these changes.

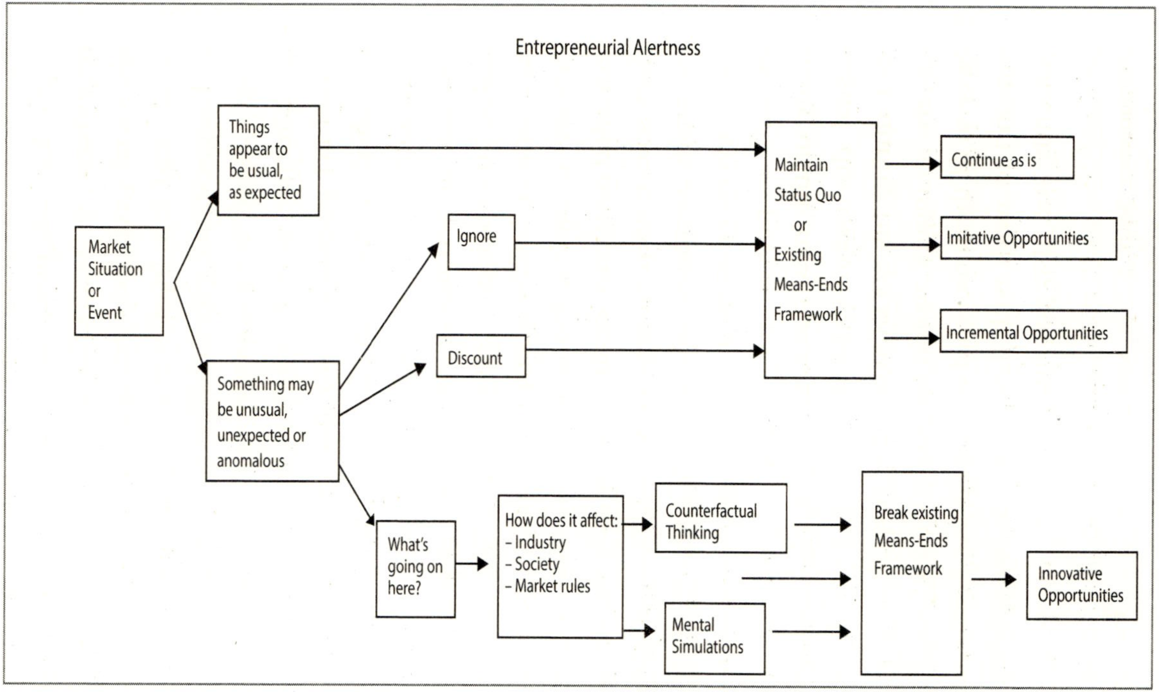

Figure 2.2 Alertness and Opportunity Identification Process*

<?>Gaglio, Connie Marie, and Jerome A. Katz. 'The psychological basis of opportunity identification: Entrepreneurial alertness'. Small Business Economics 16.2 (2001): pp. 95–111.

An alert and creative entrepreneur is aware of his networks and how important they are to identify an opportunity. Ramesh Chandra was a very social man, though his social circle was not very large. He had a close-knit family and few friends to whom he turned to for advice and suggestions. His humility and affability put others at ease making communication easy. He was vigilant, and his antennae were tuned in to read signals of change. He would act promptly if any change needed to be adopted. He relied on the strength of 'weak ties' (including casual acquaintances) as much because he believed that those were 'bridges' of information sources not necessarily contained within an individual's strong-tie network (including friends and family).[31] Casual acquaintances more likely tend to provide unique information than close friends because extended networks identify significantly more opportunities than solo entrepreneurs. This quality of network contacts enhances alertness and creativity. Ramesh Chandra would talk to everyone around him: readers, distributors, advertisers as well as people not connected to current businesses. Many of the new business that he started emerged from casual discussions with his friends as well as those he met during his social work. He was also very accessible. "Many 'strangers' would be seen visiting him in his office. Several of them received encouragement and even financial support to work with their ideas. He would listen to them patiently and also give inputs," recalls Shyam Sunder, who

[31]Granovetter, Mark S. 'The strength of weak ties'. *American Journal of Sociology* 78.6 (1973): pp. 1360–1380.

had worked with Ramesh Chandra since 1966 and retired recently.

The process of opportunity development differs based on value creation capabilities and values sought by the entrepreneur. It may represent the kind of creativity we associate with artists, 'dreamers', some designers, and inventors interested in moving proprietary knowledge in a new direction or pushing technology past its current limits.

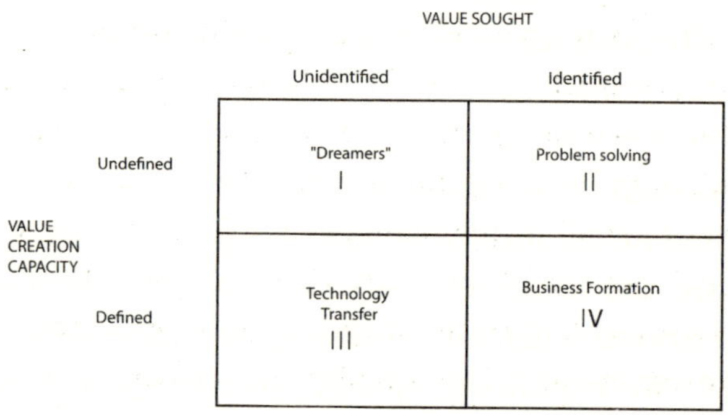

Figure 2.3 Types of Opportunities[32]

In Figure 2.3, the upper right cell – where value sought is identified but capability undefined (problems are known but solutions are not) – describes situations in which structured problem solving, including information search, occur. The goal of opportunity development in this situation is usually design of a specific product/ service to address an expressed market need. The

[32]Ardichvili, Alexander, Richard Cardozo, and Sourav Ray. 'A theory of entrepreneurial opportunity identification and development'. *Journal of Business Venturing* 18.1 (2003): pp. 105–123.

lower left cell – where value sought is unidentified but capability is defined (problems are unknown but solutions are available) – includes what we usually identify as 'technology transfer' challenges, that is, capabilities in search of an application; and idle capacity. Opportunity development here emphasises search for applications more than product/service development.

Ramesh Chandra adopted an approach that was a combination of a 'dreamer' and a 'problem solver'. He would typically pick an unmet need and find a solution to it. "One day Ramesh Chandra came to us after a visit to Sikar, a small town 115 kilometres from Jaipur,' recalls Pawan. "He asked, 'Why should the smaller towns read the same content as the large cities? The national and state news are the same to all, but the readers in Sikar should read about what is happening around them on the same day.' We explained to him that the lag between news gathering, printing and distribution causes this delay. The problem could be solved if we printed the paper locally. He simply said, 'Find a solution to print locally.' While we had the technology to print, we did not have the communication system to transmit data. No regional language newspaper had the required technology. Only two leading English dailies and the TV news channels in the country were using VSAT at that time to transmit data in real time. It required a critical mass to make an economical case for the technology. We did not have the required circulation. Yet he asked us to install the VSAT system. We were able to customise the content to the local readers. Within no time our circulation increased significantly to recover all the cost of the technology," says Pawan. Adds Sanjiv Jain, "He would ask whether the problem being faced was difficult or impossible to solve. Whenever we said it is difficult, his response would be, 'There must be a solution to it. Let's find it.' We would roll up our sleeves, and in almost all cases we found a solution that was better and economical."

In the lower right cell – where value sought is identified and capability defined (both problems and solutions are known) – opportunity development involves matching known resources and needs to form businesses that can create and deliver value. One might argue that this matrix describes a developmental progression from situations in which both problem and solution are unknown (upper left), to situations in which either the problem or solution (but not both) is known (upper right, lower left), to the situation in which both problem and solution are known (lower right). It may be hypothesised that businesses formed in cells where either problem or solution or both are unknown would be less likely to succeed than those formed where both problem and solution are known. Each of these units of the theory has several conceptual dimensions of its own.

Square Yards was founded in October 2013 to bridge the gap between NRIs and realty. Founders – the husband-wife duo investment banker and IIM-Lucknow alumnus *Tanuj Shori* and *Kanika Gupta*, a wealth manager – spotted an opportunity in NRIs. Many of them wished to invest in Indian real estate but did not have access to adequate information, support and post-transaction services. They did extensive research on real estate in different micro-markets of top 10 Indian cities and started sharing it with the NRI community. When they found the NRI demand flowing in, the company quickly expanded base in India by establishing offices in top metro cities and building relationships with top developers. The duo also created a website to facilitate end-user research on Indian residential micro-markets.

Over the next one-and-half years, Square Yards established its presence in 15 Indian cities and five countries and claimed to have gained a virtual monopoly in the NRI markets of Singapore, Hong Kong, Dubai, Abu Dhabi and London. The company achieved this through investor-friendly products such as student accommodation in Liverpool, mall redevelopment projects in Canada and car parks in Glasgow. It has grown into India's foremost proptech and real estate aggregation and transaction platform in just 6 years. It has gained 25% of market share in the last 100 days (almost 4 months) post Covid-19.[33]

The laws of interaction show that there is a relationship between social networks and alertness. The more

[33]https://yourstory.com/2015/09/square-yards-growth-story/amp

connected a person is, the higher is their alertness to potentially successful entrepreneurial opportunities. The stronger is an entrepreneur's interest in a specific area of personal interest or hobby, the higher the alertness. When interest and the social networks meet, alertness increases. There is also a continuous interaction between one's knowledge base and the opportunity development process. This interaction results in a constant learning process, described as double-loop learning, and in the development of a knowledge corridor, which leads to heightened alertness to new opportunities. Staying alert and having priorities aligned help strong leaders get ahead and embrace changing times. They process information and inputs from different sources and are never afraid to apply someone's ideas if that works in the organisation's favour. In times of crisis, Ramesh Chandra never lost a moment pondering over 'what might have been'. Instead, he quickly took note of the situation, gathered relevant data and decided what mattered most for the organisation and made decisions without any shadow of doubt.

It is equally important for leaders to stand down and listen up. A leader needs to have a strong voice but also needs to know when to listen. Keeping their ears open to find out what is going right and wrong is smart business.[34] Ramesh Chandra was always eager to know more from others. '*Aur batao* (tell me more),' would be his opening

[34]Bargh, J. A. and F. Pratto, 1986, 'Individual Construct Accessibility and Perceptual Selection', *Journal of Experimental Social Psychology* 22, pp. 293–311.

line while interacting with other people, putting them at ease and at the same time encouraging them to speak their mind. It was his way to garner maximum information, which he could use later while implementing a project. He would often have debates and discussions with his sons on a project idea. They would argue weighing the pros and cons. This helped them narrow down the challenges they feared would pose hurdles. Once the challenges were identified, the only question remained was how to tackle them. They would then team up and sort the problems piece by piece. It's a human tendency to resist something we cannot immediately accept. Ramesh Chandra was a patient listener and would listen to the smallest of concerns calmly and help reach a consensus.

However, discussions did not run into years, months or days. His deliberations would run into hours. He wouldn't sit on a decision for months. He would say, "If you want to do something, do it with focus and do it now, provided your whole heart and soul are in it. When you are focused, you can get a thing done in two hours instead of two months. *Ja ke aa sakte ho to usi domain mein rahte hue aa jao* (if you can go and come back being in the same domain, then do it).'"

Harnessing opportunities

One of the keys to identifying opportunities is taking advantage of diverse human capital having wide knowledge and skills. If opportunities are waiting to be discovered, entrepreneurs with better human capital may have better cognitive ability to recognise them, and would know where to look for a chance or gap.[35] In case opportunities are imagined or created, there would be more resources to identify or create one. Bhaskar Group's entry into radio was a well-thought plan. Their strategy was simple – enter only in their markets, their strength zones. They launched Radio FM's first station in Jaipur and created its core team from the Bhaskar team.

'*Market ko kya chahiye?* (What does the market want?),' he would ask. He had the uncanny ability to recognise a gap in the market and worked towards plugging that gap in the way the market desired. He could smell an opportunity and dive into it with a positive mindset that everything that happens is an opportunity for something new and exciting. He had a childlike craving to know everything. He would ask questions. '*Apan kya kare naya?* (What new can we do?)'. His way of gathering details about a business was to talk to as many people as he could. For instance, if he wanted to do textile business, he would talk to ten different textile business owners to gather important information – risks, growth prospects, innovations and so on. He didn't mind talking to junior-level people instead of the CFO or CEO if the need arose, says his friend Rakesh Mehra, who remembers him as fearless in business matters, one who always took calculated risks and with business acumen turned an opportunity into a

---

[35]Estrin, Saul, Tomasz Mickiewicz, and Ute Stephan. 'Human capital in social and commercial entrepreneurship'. *Journal of Business Venturing* 31.4 (2016): pp. 449–467.

successful venture. Ramesh Chandra was a leader with strong opinions and would take decisive action, but not before he had heard others' views.

Those who strive to thrive are quick to sense signals of change and act accordingly.[36] Since Ramesh Chandra was able to listen to the winds of change, he would readily adopt a new idea or market appeal, and then obtain required resources to give shape to that opportunity. Early on he sensed the importance of visual imagery in a newspaper and introduced new layouts and designs that were reader-friendly. He also emphasised on quality printing. He raised the bar for Hindi journalism by introducing words with English roots used commonly in day-to-day interaction in news reports, making news reading easier for readers.

There is a difference in how experts process information and use it to their advantage. Their schema is more developed as it is shaped by their own experience enabling them to link different inputs to arrive at critical judgements.[37] Their sense of perceiving patterns and information is sharp, and they notice anything of relevance quicker than novices.[38] Repeat entrepreneurs tend to have

---

[36]Vaghely, Ivan P., and Pierre-André Julien. 'Are opportunities recognized or constructed? : An information perspective on entrepreneurial opportunity identification.' *Journal of Business Venturing* 25.1 (2010): pp. 73–86.
[37]Glaser, R., and Chi, M. T. H. (1988). Overview. In M. T. H. Chi, R. Glaser, and M. J. Farr (Eds.), The Nature of Expertise (pp. xv-xxviii). Hillsdale, NJ: Erlbaum
[38]Lord, Robert G., and Karen J. Maher. 'Alternative information-processing models and their implications for theory, research, and practice.' *Academy of Management Review* 15.1 (1990): pp. 9–28.

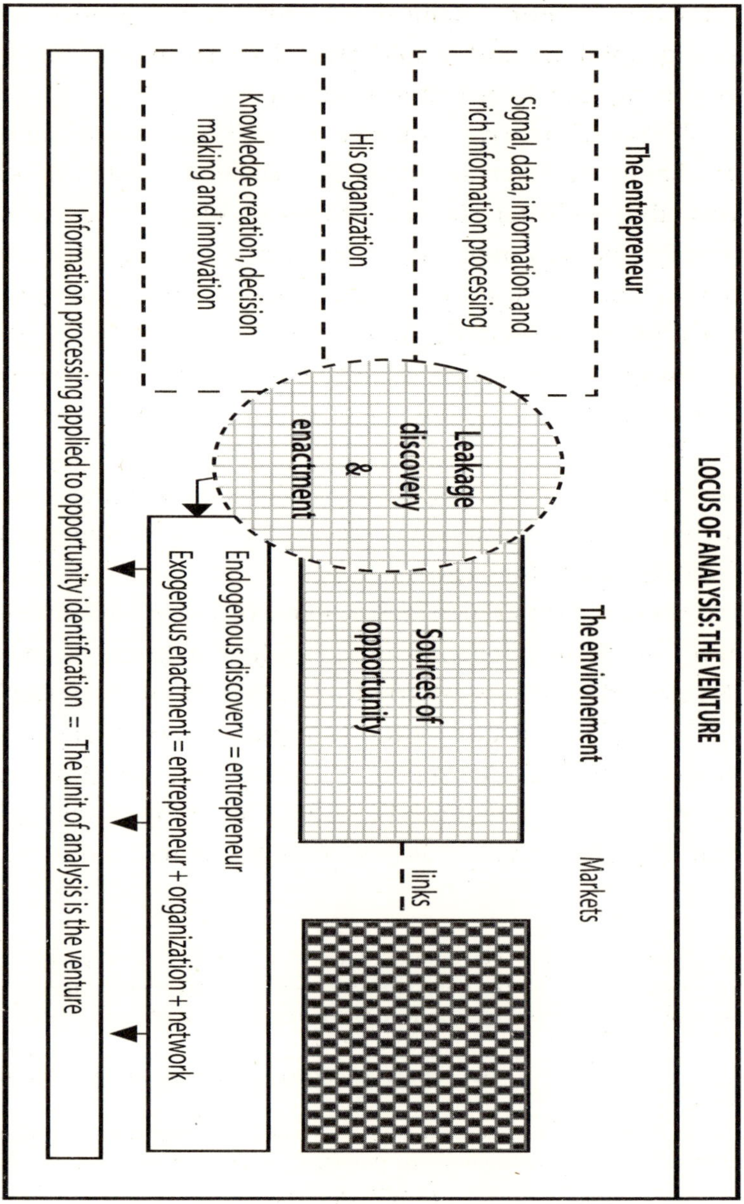
LOCUS OF ANALYSIS: THE VENTURE
The entrepreneur
Signal, data, information and rich information processing
His organization
Knowledge creation, decision making and innovation
Leakage discovery & enactment
The environement
Sources of opportunity
Markets
links
Endogenous discovery = entrepreneur
Exogenous enactment = entrepreneur + organization + network
Information processing applied to opportunity identification = The unit of analysis is the venture

Figure 2.4

better developed opportunity identification schema that gives direction to their attention, expectations and interpretations of market stimuli as well as enable them to generate ideas.[39] They are able to 'connect the dots' between changes or events that seem unrelated and find meaningful patterns more easily than inexperienced entrepreneurs.[40]

Udaan is a Bengaluru-based online platform in B2B segment to connect retailers, wholesalers, traders and manufacturers through a mobile app. Run by Hiveloop Technology Pvt. Ltd, it is a special initiative for small and medium businesses in India. The main idea was to connect wholesalers, traders, retailers and manufacturers on a single platform via a mobile app. Users can access active trends and other premium B2B trade features via this app. Udaan was founded by former Flipkart employees Vaibhav Gupta, Sujeet Kumar and Amod Malviya. They spotted a gap in the supply chain angle. Since internet penetration was not there, goods dealers did not use the internet. But with internet now penetrating villages, it's been easier to reach data to them. The founders analysed

[39]Gaglio, Connie Marie. 'The role of mental simulations and counterfactual thinking in the opportunity identification process.' *Entrepreneurship Theory and Practice* 28.6 (2004): pp. 533–552.

[40]Baron, Robert A., and Michael D. Ensley. 'Opportunity recognition as the detection of meaningful patterns: Evidence from comparisons of novice and experienced entrepreneurs.' Management science 52.9 (2006): pp. 1331–1344.

> the market for the first six months in 2016. They went on the ground, spoke to retailers, suppliers and tried to understand their roles. They launched their beta in November 2016 after all the research. For seven months – it was used by … retailers, manufacturers and then a year later in 2017, the company was started.[41]

"Many of us saw DB's foray into the shopping mall as pure diversification. Ramesh Chandra had his own ways of linking the businesses," says Sanjiv Jain, a chartered accountant hired to develop the malls with no prior experience in the domain. 'Advertising is driven by the brands presents in the local markets. We have only those brands that sell through traditional channels, simply because there is no retail space for bigger brands in Bhopal. Also, media planning for these large advertisers are planned with national-level data on CDI and newspaper readership. Local presence of their own stores would drive advertising. Since we would have them as tenants, we could get a larger share of their advertising,' he remembers the discussion with Ramesh Chandra.

Since repeat entrepreneurs have years of experience to draw on, they may tend to take shortcuts. This can sometimes make them overconfident that they know enough or they can elicit sufficient data from very little information.[42] This

[41]https://lapaas.com/udaan-business-model-detailed-case-study/

[42]Tversky, Amos, and Daniel Kahneman. 'Judgment under Uncertainty: Heuristics and Biases: Biases in judgments reveal some heuristics of thinking

can prove to be a hindrance in recognising new avenues. Failure can limit an individual's performance as they lose confidence in their ability.[43] Ramesh Chandra, however, was different. He had faced both failures and successes that had enriched his cognitive diversity, enabling him to plan his future ventures. For him failure was a 'clear signal' to conduct a post-mortem to understand what led to the failure; this aided the development of his schema. Sudhir remembers him as a big risk taker who would gamble but only with the money in his pocket, money earned by him. He understood what he would lose if he put money into the stock market, lottery or a start-up or unicorn business. He would say, 'Our core business is doing very well, so we will continue with that.' He made it very clear that if you decide to pursue a business venture, the potential loss would be limited to the amount you invest in building it. But, if you choose not to proceed, you wouldn't incur that specific financial risk. That is why his moves were very calculated, one that was influenced by his own cognitive ability and not by any presentations. He would do calculations based on his gut feeling and be absolutely hands-on with numbers like a mini computer.

Ramesh Chandra had political links, but unlike other media persons he never leveraged them for his personal gains. Sometime after he decided to expand beyond newspapers, he made several attempts at entering other

under uncertainty'. *Science* 185.4157 (1974): pp. 1124–1131.
[43]Baron, 1998.

sectors like oil, sugar, cement, refinery, realty and textiles. Some failed, some succeeded. He tried to buy sick plants in government auctions but did not succeed because either the government would change policy or the government itself would change in a particular state. In some cases, he was asked to deposit a substantial sum in the party fund in lieu of getting approval to start a plant in the state. When the time came to put the money in the fund, circumstances shifted due to a change in government or a transition in leadership. His plans would get caught in political tangles. Following setbacks in dealing with different state governments, Ramesh Chandra decided not to deal with governments at all.

The rise of the group shows its founder's overall game-plan, how he reached prospective consumers and turned them into customers. "A people person, Ramesh Chandra would go to the market, meet people and talk to them to get the pulse of the market. He would gather related data, have all the necessary numbers figured out in his mind and was ready to go. He wasn't a geek but always had the numbers calculated in his mind before a take-off," says Girish.

For Ramesh Chandra, nobody was too big or too small in front of the organisation and its purpose. He was driven and so was his team. His passion was the driving force behind his conquests. Failures, few and far between, never intimidated him. He would move on picking up the thread of trade as something new and exciting beckoned him. Pawan sees him as a leader who used to make the new purpose so huge that all other hurdles seemed small and irrelevant. "Making that purpose bigger got everybody together and aligned, so that none had even an iota of doubt about their ability. It's just like India going to play the cricket world cup and the team getting ready to play it with all enthusiasm, saying "*hum jeet ke aayenge* (We will be victorious)."

3

The Big Picture

19 December 1996. Jaipur. *Dainik Bhaskar* entered Rajasthan with a bang. It launched in the Pink City of Jaipur with an eye on gaining the No. 2 position in the market, as *Rajasthan Patrika* was the leader there. Its target was to sell 50,000 copies on the first day. To achieve this goal, it conducted a survey of 1.25 lakh households in the city to know what people preferred to read. The Bhaskar team then made a newspaper prototype based on people's feedback and went back to them to show what kind of content the newspaper would contain. The households surveyed were offered the option of an advance subscription at ₹1.50 (the newsstand price was ₹2), and a refund if they did not like the content and wanted to discontinue. *Dainik Bhaskar* launched in Jaipur on 19 December 1996, at the No. 1 position by selling 172,347 copies.

> There's no defining action or miracle that builds a great organisation. In fact, it rather feels like one is pushing a giant flywheel. One keeps pushing it till it completes one turn. It moves faster as the push becomes stronger. Then a point comes when breakthrough happens. One keeps building with each turn, investing in his efforts. The flywheel continues to move forward with unstoppable pace. This is the way greatness is built. The approach needs a very clear and unwavering focus. Like the Stockdale Paradox 'Retain faith that you will prevail in the end, regardless of difficulties', leaders take 'series of good decisions consistent with a simple, coherent concept called the Hedgehog Approach. A simple and clear concept that flows from deep understanding about the intersection of three circles of what you are deeply passionate about, what you can be the best in the world at, and what best drives your economic or resource engine.[44]

The 'big picture' is increasingly becoming an indispensable tool. Firms recognise the value of a bird's eye view for customers and its competitive advantage over others. Very few can see the overall dynamics of an industry. Planning a strategy and identifying factors of competition are not easy. What is envisioned in the first draft usually changes

---

[44]Jim Collins, Good to Great: *Why Some Companies Make the Leap and Others Don't*, Harper Business, 2001.

by the final draft.[45] To break away from the competition, one needs to adopt a structured process for drawing and discussing a strategy canvas that pushes a company's strategy toward a blue ocean (this is a business strategy that focuses on carving out a fresh market space—a 'blue ocean'—where competition is minimal or nonexistent rather than competing in an existing market). The process builds on the paths of creating blue oceans and involves a lot of visual stimulation in order to unlock people's creativity.[46]

Building the big picture

That the Bhaskar Group's expansion has been consistent with the change in times suggests its leader's efforts were well spent on macro-management. Ramesh Chandra always strived to see the big picture to understand the market nuances. Based on his past experiences, just as he could sense problems arising, he could also find solutions because he had successfully implemented them himself elsewhere. He had a big-picture view because he was able to assemble pieces of data gathered from different sources. It gave him access to the entire market that yielded him a unique insight. This perspective meant he could see the forest and the trees while others could only see trees. Information, significant or otherwise, has

---

[45]Elsbeth Johnson, How Leaders can Focus on the Big Picture, www.hbr.org, 9 November 2016.

[46]Chan W Kim and Renee Mauborgne, *Focus on the Big Picture Not the Numbers*, Chapter 4, Blue Ocean Strategy, Harvard Business Publishing.

value only when assembled with other pieces of data to reveal something new.

A new big picture can have extensive impact on customer behaviour and industry dynamics. For instance, the book publishing industry was completely changed in 1895 after *The Bookman,* the literary magazine, introduced monthly ranking of fiction sales. It became the first national best-seller list in the United States. Today, the *New York Times* best-seller list compiles data on book sales through different sources and publishes a big picture for readers. People value what others are reading. The lists drive individual reader behaviour, boosting book sales.

The ability to see the big picture is linked with competitive strategising. Strategists are always looking for new inventions or technologies to get a big-picture view in order to have an edge over their competitors.

When asked what prompts them to seek out blue oceans and introduce change, executives usually say that it takes a highly determined leader or a serious crisis. Getting the wake-up call is only the first step. The next step is to send a team into the field, putting the members face-to-face with what they must make sense of: how people use or don't use their products or services. This step may seem obvious, but organisations often outsource this part of the strategy-making process.[47] They rely on reports that other people have put together. Best practice suggests that one should never rely on the eyes of other people.

[47]Judge William, The Big Picture, *Building Organisational Capacity for Change*, Harvard Business Publishing, 1 February 2011.

The Four Steps of Visualizing Strategy

1. Visual awakening	2. Visual exploration	3. Visual strategy fair	4. Visual communication
• Compare your business with your competitors' by drawing your "as is" strategy canvas. • See where your strategy needs to change.	• Go into the field to explore the six paths to creating blue oceans. • Observe the distinctive advantages of alternative products and sevices. • See which factors you should eliminate, create, or change.	• Draw your "to be" strategy canvas based on insights from field observations. • Get feedback on alternative strategy canvases from customers, competitors customers, and noncustomers. • Use feedback to build the best "to be" future strategy.	• Distribute your before-and-after strategic profiles on one page for easy comparison. • Support only those projects and operational moves that allow your company to close the gaps to actualize the new strategy.

Figure 3.1 Building a Big Picture*

*Chan W Kim and Renee Mauborgne, Focus on the Big Picture Not the Numbers, Chapter 4, Blue Ocean Strategy, Harvard Business Publishing.

Divya Bhaskar, the Gujarati edition of *Dainik Bhaskar* launched in 2003, had become the leading daily in Ahmedabad within two years of its launch, its readership reaching very near to that of the prevailing leader *Gujarat Samachar*. However, a few years later the company found itself in a saturated market scenario. Ramesh Chandra, who had given his sons charge of the newspaper business to pursue his passion for expansion in different sectors and social service, stepped in to see for himself the actual picture – there's no substitute for assessing a situation for yourself. Great strategists never see from other's eyes. They get into the field and challenge the boundaries of the competition. In this case, Ramesh Chandra's insight helped identify the uncovered market in the state, which his team thought had been covered. "This allowed him to see what was invisible to the others. He met distributors and had a dialogue with them. He re-evaluated the company's strategy and got them involved. It transformed the company's revenue graph, and within three months it witnessed a jump of 20 per cent in circulation,' recalls Girish.

Re-evaluating a strategy can benefit the dialogue among different business units and transform a company's business portfolio from red to blue. When business units present their strategy canvases to one another, they deepen their understanding of the other businesses in the corporate portfolio. Moreover, the process also fosters the transfer of strategic best practices across units.

Participative leadership

The organisation under Ramesh Chandra aimed for participative leadership with 'change as the only constant'. To macro-manage, he dwelt on questions such as 'Why the organisation exists?', 'What can it offer to customers?' and 'How do people in the organisation behave with its customers, stakeholders and each other?' He would meditate on these ideas in his mind to find the answers or understand if there was a need to refine them.[48]

(i) *What new can we do?* When deciding what he wanted, like a certain position in the market or a new launch, Ramesh Chandra reflected on what new he could do to add value and earn profit. This forced him to think through options.

(ii) *Invest with the money in one's pocket.* When organisations have enough money, they tend to 'choose everything' leading to underperformance and losses putting an organisation's capability under strain. Ramesh Chandra always took calculated risks, only with the money in his pocket, his own earned money. He would calculate loss, if incurred in the process of doing a business, and only then moved ahead.

(iii) *Talk to the unusual suspects.* To get the complete picture, Ramesh Chandra talked to people outside his

[48]Elsbeth Johnson, *How Leaders can Focus on the Big Picture*, www.hbr.org, 9 November 2016.

close circle. Often, they would tell him something that he didn't know. Such people helped him test whether he had the best answers to macro questions. He always had a lot of questions: Will it work? If not, what do I have to do new for it to turn out in a certain way? He always challenged himself and those working closely with him. He would go to great lengths to have new information.

(iv) *Exist at the macro and micro-levels simultaneously.* Ramesh Chandra never limited his thought process. It was beautiful how he used to look at the big picture. He would go to the top at 30,000 feet and come down to the ground to get a complete view. He would get a ground view, look at the team, align with them on the ground and then immediately go to the top at 30,000 feet. He would say, 'I can't stay at 30,000 feet all the time and remain on the ground all the time. I have to keep shunting between the two.' It is very difficult to maintain both the views, but he did that as he trusted people on the ground. 'If you don't trust people on the ground, you will keep wondering at 30,000 ft. what must be happening at ground zero,' he believed. He never needed to stay at ground zero. "He worked with a lot of clarity, and he always expected clarity from others as well. Once he was convinced that others had absolute clarity on things that he wanted to convey to them, he would step back," says Sudhir.

Trust building for Ramesh Chandra was a mutual process. Once he picked the person to lead an initiative, he would leave the matter to the person totally. "I still do not remember a single incident when Ramesh Chandra sent someone to inquire about how I was working. I had full freedom to take decisions regarding the mall and was never questioned by Ramesh Chandra,' recalls Sanjay Jain. 'Once given charge, he would expect, without saying it, all of us to give the best and to succeed in whatever we did. Typical of him, almost every day I would get a call from him while I was having breakfast. His only words used to be 'Aur batao…' and everything unfolded. Next day, the same words. You knew that he was expecting things to be accomplished. If the issues remained unresolved for a few days, you also knew that he would simply say 'do this' or meet so-and-so, and the problem would be resolved.'

Building capacity for organisational change

Capable leaders and involved mid-management are oriented towards unleashing the power of lateral leadership, which is concerned with getting things done across organisational units and functional areas of expertise. The hierarchical organisation will always be with us, but the power of hierarchical authority is diminishing. In its place is the power of influence without authority; in other words, lateral leadership is emerging. Crisis situations demonstrate this power equation quite clearly. When a crisis occurs, people often self-organise into social groups that do amazing things in inexplicably short amounts of time. The trick here is to enable the organisation to self-organise.

Organisational capacity for change is dependent largely on the human capital within the firm.[49] Trustworthy leadership and trusting followers are oriented towards producing organisational trust to the greatest extent possible. Organisational trust refers to the ability of members of an organisation to put their lives and well-being at risk in service to the well-being of the overall organisation. It is an indicator of how much trust frontline workers put on middle managers and senior executives to watch out for their interests. Similarly, it addresses how much top executives trust middle managers and frontline workers to do their jobs well.

Ramesh Chandra didn't meet frontline people always because he didn't have time to come down from 30,000 feet to be with them and interact with them all the time. However, whenever he met them he would elicit important information from them. He didn't spend a lot of time energising them as he considered it to be the job of the team at the top levels. When he found a problem with the frontline, he would do their health check to determine if there were lapses on the part of the seniors.

---

[49]Buono, Anthony F., and Kenneth W. Kerber. 'Creating a sustainable approach to change: Building organisational change capacity.' *SAM Advanced Management Journal* 75.2 (2010): pp. 4–21.

He would correct that. Pawan says, "Many a time, seniors whom we brothers thought were aligned with our line of thought, did not further align with their subordinates and frontline workers. They would lack the drive to motivate their juniors'. Ramesh Chandra would always say, "Ninety-nine per cent cases *mein seniors mein jazba tha hi nahi*' ('In ninety-nine per cent of the cases, the seniors did not have passion'). So, who's responsible?" he would ask and then point out to his sons, "You are responsible because you didn't do a health check." He always used to read the minds of the seniors even without the need to ask them questions. It was evident to him when they took three steps backwards. When leaders believed they had established a rapport with senior executives, there were still occasions when they were mistaken. He used to emphasize that senior executives should not be held responsible. "*Aap pehli jyot ho* (you are the first light), if you (his sons) become weak, *diya kaise jalegi* (how will the lamp burn)?"

People committed to the organization's mission are its biggest resource. Ramesh Chandra was an ideas man, not a project man. He needed people to implement his ideas. He was lucky to have a good team that he built by picking the right people without much hassle of 'reference checks that companies have to do today'. As Collins has rightly said, '*The right people can often attract money, but money by itself can never attract the right people. Money is a commodity; talent is not. Time and talent can often compensate for lack of money, but money cannot ever compensate for lack of the right people.*' Great companies focus on getting and hanging on to the right people, those who are productive, those who are self-motivated and self-disciplined, those who wake up every day, compulsively driven to do the best they can because it is simply part of their DNA.

Ramesh Chandra clearly understood the importance of working with the right people and seeing it they fit into the organization's culture. You can do one of two things – hire the right people or make them the right people; either you align with them or make them align with you. A person's DNA, culture, background, and upbringing can influence whether he'll culturally do what he is required to do. For example, if one doesn't drink, you can't force him to drink or you can't make a smoker quit smoking. Cultural compatibility is important. So, Ramesh Chandra would always create teams that were culturally suited to Bhaskar. His people came from humble backgrounds, they had struggled a lot – nothing was served to them on a platter. Even if someone was from a rich background, he had done a lot of hard work to reach where he was at that moment.

Following in the footsteps of their father, the Agarwal brothers always try to build a good team and have laid down four principles as a value system based on four key characteristics of their father.

1. Be a Trendsetter: An action or a step has to be different from the past.
2. Remain Connected to the Ground: Regular ground

checks.

3. Become Analytical: Data is very important. Get data of the past and always look at data of the future.
4. Stay Result-Oriented: As the owner of the project, keep checking progress every hour.

Zoom In and Zoom Out

How leaders view the world may aid or impede their ability to make good strategic decisions. One may zoom in to get a close look at details or zoom out to see the big picture. Zooming in and out, i.e., having both the worm's- and the bird's-eye views have good as well as bad aspects. Leaders need to have multiple perspectives to understand the complete, bigger picture since it enhances their chances of being right.

> Of the 14 Amazon's leadership principles that are part of the company's ethos, according to Jeff Bezos the one that surprises people the most is the fourth principle – 'be right, a lot'. Good leaders are right a lot. You're not going to be right all the time, but I think with practice, you can be right more often. People who are right a lot, they listen a lot, and people who are right a lot, change their mind a lot. Most people usually gather data to strengthen their beliefs and ignore opposing opinions, but not 'people who are right' because they do the opposite.

> People who are right seek to dis-confirm their most profoundly held convictions, which is very unnatural for humans. Humans mostly, as we go about life, we're very selective in the evidence we let seep into us, and we like to observe the evidence that confirms our pre-existing belief. 'Sometimes when you get new data, you change your mind. Sometimes you don't get new data, and you just re-analyse the situation, and you realise it's more complicated than you initially thought it was, and you change your mind.'[50]

Some people prefer to see things up close, others from afar. There should be vantage points for leaders to examine scenarios from different viewpoints. Effective leaders zoom in and zoom out, as was the case with Ramesh Chandra. He effortlessly switched between high-level strategic thinking and hands-on operational tasks! Zooming in brings the details into sharp focus. A close-in perspective is often found in relationship-intensive settings, where human talent is the primary asset. Relying heavily on personal instinct and interpersonal deals without a wider perspective or a long-term rationale can prove perilous. An overly personal approach can also make managers quick to perceive slights, whether or not they're real. Self-reflection is a learning process that requires a distant perspective on one's own behaviour, in context. An obsession with self is reinforced

[50]https://www.cnbc.com/2019/10/11/jeff-bezos-amazon-leadership-principle-that-surprises-people.html.

by zooming in, but self-awareness stems from zooming out, which is essential to big-picture decision-making. When people are far removed from a situation, they can map the whole territory before taking action. They see events as examples of general patterns rather than as idiosyncratic or personal incidents. They put things in context and stress principles. It helps people see the map and stay focused on larger principles. There are leaders who work in both directions – zoom in and zoom out. If in a crisis, they zoom in to see problems even as they zoom out to look for similar situations, causes and principles or policies that will help prevent it to recur.

The idea of zooming in and out suggests that leaders don't have to divide the world into extremes – 'idiosyncratic or structural, situational or strategic, emotional or contextual'. It's not about choosing one over the other but to keep learning from both perspectives. Ramesh Chandra's entrepreneurial genius was that he could often gauge the outcome of his decisions while putting details and events into a sequential order, zooming in and out quickly while being in the same domain. That dynamic capability was the essence of his strategic thinking. Zooming helped him to respond to situations before they become crises. That way he could accept new opportunities while working with principles that build sustainable institutions for the long run. Leaders should make room to zoom.

Procter & Gamble Former Chairman, President and CEO, Robert McDonald headed a global public company with a long-established culture. With an eye on profits, his focus was always on what will support the sustainability of the company and its values. He appreciated cultural differences and never personalised issues because he called himself 'a steward of an institution that must endure beyond him'. Daniel Vasella, Former Chairman and CEO of pharmaceutical giant Novartis, was both a psychiatrist by training – which made him able to zoom in on the emotional state of the people around him – and a strategist with a theory of industry change that guided divestitures, acquisitions, and internal restructuring. He stressed personal values as well as global trends. Indra Nooyi, PepsiCo's Former CEO, blends a big-picture view of principles guiding the company, such as the need for transformation in food and beverage companies to promote improved health, with an ability to zoom in on the details of budget allocations for current business lines. Nooyi had defined new roles (such as a chief science officer) and new structures (for instance, the Global Nutrition Group, linked to central R&D) that helped the previously decentralised organisation both zoom out to a global perspective and zoom in on local differences.[51]

[51]Rosabeth Moss Kanter, 'Zoom In, Zoom Out'. *Harvard Business Review*, March 2011, pp. 2–6.

Ramesh Chandra would take action keeping the future in mind, and his farsightedness yielded rich dividends as is evident in how his organisation expanded and diversified keeping with the times. He would always say, "I plant trees and not seasonal crops because trees yield fruits for a long time, for generations to come." Everything he did was an investment for generations to come. Whatever he did changed the lives of generations, changed journalism, changed people and the way they engaged with media stakeholders in many ways. He could redefine everything. Since he was a great learner, he would go to the last-mile person to understand any new idea or business. When he had to start a solvent business, he would speak to first-level engineers or sales managers and not the CEOs. He would talk to the owner or CEO in the end. He learnt from his mistakes. In case of any gap or lapse, he would try not to repeat that same mistake. He would say 'whatever you do should have a purpose'. There was objectivity to the madness.

Purpose to implementation

Purpose defines leadership, shapes goals, offers a direction and gives meaning to action. Less than 20 per cent of leaders have a strong sense of individual purpose. Less than that can translate their purpose into a concrete statement.[52] They may be able to clearly articulate their

[52]Craig Nick Scot Snook, 'From Purpose to Impact'. *Harvard Business Review*, May 2014, pp. 4–9.

organisation's mission: Think of Google's 'To organise the world's information and make it universally accessible and useful,' or Charles Schwab's 'A relentless ally for the individual investor'. But when asked to describe their own purpose, leaders typically fall back on something generic and nebulous: 'Help others excel', 'ensure success' or "empower my people'. Just as problematic, hardly any of them have a clear plan for translating purpose into action.[53] As a result, they limit their aspirations and often fail to achieve their most ambitious professional and personal goals.

PURPOSE STATEMENT[54]

FROM BAD	TO GOOD
Lead new markets department to achieve exceptional business results	Eliminate 'chaos'
Be a driver in the infrastructure business that allows each person to achieve their needed outcomes while also mastering the new drivers of our business as I balance my family and work demands	Bring water and power to the 2 billion people who do not have it

[53]Heifetz Roland, Alexande Grashow and Martin Linsky, *The Practice of Adaptive Leadership*, Harvard Business Press.
[54]Craig Nick Scot Snook, 'From Purpose to Impact'. *Harvard Business Review*, May 2014, pp. 4–9.

FROM BAD	TO GOOD
Continually and consistently develop and facilitate the growth and development of myself and others leading to great performance	With tenacity, create brilliance

Finding one's leadership purpose is not easy. If it were that simple, we would all be living it every day of our life. We are constantly badgered with what-to-dos and what-not-to-dos by our bosses, parents, advertisers and management gurus. They keep reminding us how to improve ourselves to lead an empowered and smarter life. In such a world, it is not easy to figure out who we are, let alone our purpose. But it is also true once we know who we are, everything else follows naturally. Ramesh Chandra would make definite plans about the future. He had a vision '*hamein itna bada hona hai, itni badi company create karni hai*' ('we have to become this big, create a company of this size'). But he would not make plans for next 20 years. He would plan for 2 to 5 years. '*Yeh apne ko karna hai, ise dekhna chahiye aur ise dekho ab*' ('We have to do this, we should consider this and so let's do it'). However, he never planned for the short term as he never believed in short gains; he definitely had the big picture in his mind.

Those who have followed Elon Musk's career know that very early in life he had developed a set of goals and has worked meticulously to reach those goals. His tireless focused approach is the reason that he has been able to create mid-priced EVs [electric vehicles] for mass market. Those inside the auto industry and those following auto trends are aware of Tesla's master plan, a three-part strategy to bring EV to the market. Long-term planning is a rarity in auto industry but it has served Tesla and Elon well. One of the keys to creating a big picture, he relies on feedback, both positive and negative. However, he emphasises more on negative inputs, that too, from friends. 'Don't tell me what you like, tell me what you don't like,' he tells his friends. He says, 'You really need to coax people for negative feedback. They may be wrong, but you know that it's coming from a good place if the feedback is coming from a friend or someone who is not your enemy. It's also important to reason from first principles rather than by analogy because reason from principles can boil things down to the most fundamental truths as it requires more mental energy.' According to a Wharton School professor, Tesla's Master Plan was like the Apollo programme – very specific about the goal, but didn't specify the details of how to reach it. He says this kind of long-term planning allows teams to change their tactics as required, without losing sight of the goal, and this may be the best way to get things done during periods of uncertainty and change.

For Ramesh Chandra, his purpose was his enterprise he was so driven about. The magic lay not in what he did, but how and why he did it – the strengths and passions he brought to the table were infectious. He believed that brand is an outcome of the relationship between consumers and the product. He encouraged the practice of experimentation, which his sons have been employing even after him. It's what set him apart from other leaders of his time. As Girish says, "It is not about a name, but giving the right product to your consumer, and then everything emerges on its own. For him, for the content to be relevant, it had to have as much personalisation as possible." Adds Bhatnagar, "Even while reporting an accident, he would like the names of the person affected and any other relevant details and not simply stating that an accident has happened. Ground connect was key to any content".

PURPOSE-TO-IMPACT PLANNING	TRADITIONAL DEVELOPMENT PLANNING
Uses meaningful, purpose-infused language	Uses standard business language
Is focused on strengths to realise career aspirations	Is focused on weaknesses to address performance
Elicits a statement of leadership purpose that explains how they will lead	States a business- or career-driven goal

PURPOSE-TO-IMPACT PLANNING	TRADITIONAL DEVELOPMENT PLANNING
Sets incremental goals related to living your leadership purpose	Measures success using metrics tied to the firm's mission and goals
Focuses on the future, working backward	Focuses on the present, working forward
Is unique to you; addresses who you are as a leader	Is generic; addresses the job or role
Takes a holistic view of work and family	Ignores goals and responsibilities outside the office

Figure 3: Purpose to Impact Planning[55]

For leaders, action matters more than their words. Simply writing down the mission statement does not clarify their purpose. They must live the purpose to leave an impact on the world. For Ramesh Chandra, work was life, and it translated into successful ventures. His understanding of what motivated him increased his ability to achieve big goals in his life. Clarity of purpose, knowing what can and can't be done, using purpose-to-impact plans and a start-to-finish approach – Ramesh Chandra's line of action as a leader entailed these. He lived his purpose fully everywhere, whether at work or with his family.

While setting goals and slotting time-frames for them, Ramesh Chandra would create a core team that would

[55]Craig Nick Scot Snook, 'From Purpose to Impact'. *Harvard Business Review*, May 2014, pp. 4–9.

usually comprise his sons and close associates. It would help him stay focused and true to his goals. "We were all ready to launch our Jaipur edition. The market response went beyond out estimates. We had to print almost 1.5 times more copies. This required installing an additional machine. I had come from established organisations that would take 40 to 60 days to plan and another 60 days to get the machine operative. We did everything in 48 hours, including the civil construction, and printed the required copies. I had never witnessed such a purpose- and implementation-driven exercise earlier," says Bhatnagar.

4

The Balancing Act

May 2006, Jaipur. The Bhaskar Group launched 93.4 MY FM Radio in Jaipur. The organisation's diversification strategy was clear: it aimed to determine the business in which the group should invest and the market where it should be established Though a completely independent vertical, radio was a sequential step – a strategic choice to expand the business after studying the market and understanding the existing organisational product and market base. Ramesh Chandra had an insatiable appetite and, though daunting, he launched edition after edition in twelve states, turning a humble start into a venture worth thousands of crores of rupees.

Expansion is important to develop a business. Any new venture, related or unrelated to the main business, requires innovation and fresh ideas, and implementing fresh ideas requires an open mind. Ramesh Chandra was always ready to venture in the unknown, in a new market with his new product. Meetings with the likes of Dhirubhai Ambani spurred on his ambition to venture into new territories, taking on challenges without any fear. New ad regime and innovative marketing strategies spelled success for the group. Ramesh Chandra had a knack for getting the balance right, and though he failed a few times, his business flourished.

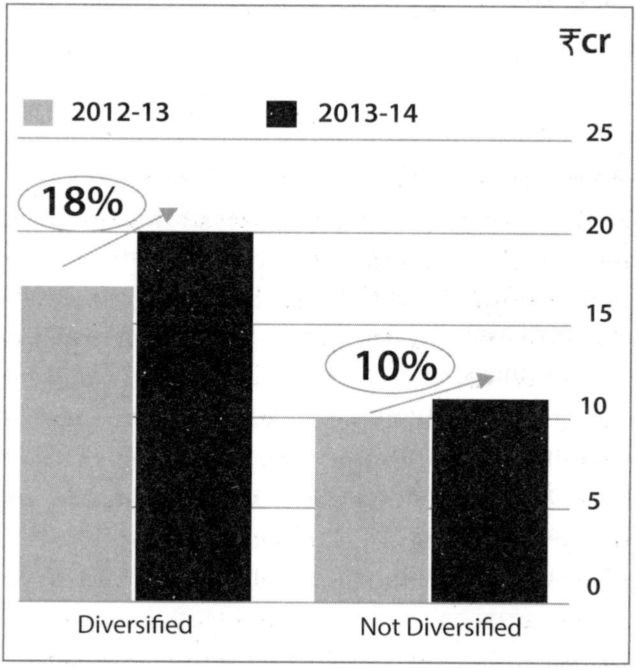

Diversification strategy can be viewed as a reflection of corporate strategy, and most are driven by the search for synergy or an inquiry into what complements the organisation's existing product/market-related resources.[56] Average sales of MSMEs with a diversified product/service, customer and geography base tend to grow higher than the growth chalked up by players with limited diversification. Diversification enables an MSME to have a stable revenue stream and, therefore, heightens its competitive advantage vis-à-vis industry peers. Also, MSMEs with a diversified profile seem to have a longer track record (more than 10 years) and were backed by their promoters' extensive experience, compared with those with a non-diversified profile. The key factors that enable MSMEs to excel are the track record and promoters' experience.

A widely accepted classification of diversification strategy includes seven categories: single business, dominant vertical, dominant constrained, dominant linked unrelated, related constrained, related linked, and unrelated business.[57] These categories can be assessed according to the product/market relatedness of businesses at the corporate level. Corporate entrepreneurship strategy, on the other hand, is not about the product/market relatedness and the synergy with the existing business but rather about emergence, creation and newness. Corporate entrepreneurship and diversification still cannot be considered totally distinct.[58]

---

[56]Bostjan Antoncic, 'Impacts of Diversification and Corporate Entrepreneurship Strategy Making on Growth And Profitability: A Normative Model'. *Journal of Enterprising Culture*, Vol. 14, No. 1 (March 2006), pp. 49–63.

[57]Rumelt, R.P. (1974). *Strategy, structure, and economic performance*. Cambridge: Harvard University Press.

[58]Gartner, W. B., Bird, B. J. and Starr, J. A. (1992). 'Acting as if: Differentiating Entrepreneurial from Organisational Behavior'. *Entrepreneurship Theory and Practice*, 16 (3): pp. 13–31.

Changing the diversification focus, as well as entering new, unfamiliar businesses in terms of product/markets, can be considered corporate entrepreneurial activities of existing firms since they represent departures from the customary way of doing business.

Phase I: Early steps

Though it is daunting, expansion is essential not only for the development of a business but also for its stable future. It encourages innovation and progress, as well as increases employment opportunities. After establishing *Danik Bhaskar* in Madhya Pradesh, Ramesh Chandra mulled spreading his wings in other states as an industrialist. He went all out to give *Dainik Bhaskar* a makeover to make it the number one business. NM Shukla, a consultant with experience in setting up operations for companies like Eicher in Madhya Pradesh, recalls, “I met Rameshji at a business event. A few days later he came to my office and started enquiring about different opportunities. He had already established *Dainik Bhaskar* in Madhya Pradesh. Business was generating surplus, which he wanted to invest in some other business. We deliberated for days. Since I had worked with a company that had a national presence, he found the discussions enriching. I found him to be sincere and inquisitive. I also realised that he had established a newspaper business but did not know much about other sectors. Also, his ideas were coming mostly from discussions with people in Bhopal. With the funds he had, a greenfield project would be very risky. We found that we could get into sectors where the government was selling units that had turned sick."

His first move was to buy industries auctioned by state governments. However, diversifying in other sectors involved dealing with different state governments, which didn't prove quite fruitful. "We found it fraught with a lot of uncertainties. It also involved dealing with politicians and bureaucrats in a different way. Ramesh Chandra hesitated and withdrew from that path after encountering a couple of experiences that conflicted with his principles. He then shifted his focus to his home state. Agribusiness, especially oilseeds, was a good opportunity around Indore," says Shukla.

Diversification is a challenging decision, as it is a high-stakes game, both rewards and risks being on the higher side. When Ramesh Chandra looked at diversification, he did not think about what his organisation excelled at; he thought about how better his organisation could perform than its competitors. "His ideas would also come from this constant endeavour to give back to the society. His decision to build a mall in Bhopal was also a way to give back to the city that had given him so much. One fine morning we were called for a meeting and asked to explore how we could have a shopping mall that was equal to if not better than other malls in Mumbai, Delhi or Bengaluru. I was given this task. None of us had any experience in the business. So we learnt from the best in the world. We visited Dubai and other cities. We hired the services of one of the leading consultants from South Africa. Even after more than 10 years, it is one of the most successful malls in Bhopal," recalls Sanjay Jain.

Phase II: Bhaskar Industry as a diversified company

It is crucial for a firm to know its strengths before trying to apply them elsewhere. Ramesh Chandra was first and foremost a media man. After seeing his core business of newspaper reach a secure position, the restless businessman in him began eyeing other sectors. "His heart, though," says Shukla, "oscillated between diversifying in unrelated business and remaining in the core sector."

In order to grow, organisations need to create, evolve and sustain new ideas. 'We must have our eyes set simultaneously on the old and the new in order to achieve success, which is attained only when there is a mix of old and new organisational characteristics, a blend of both the worlds achieved through balancing acts,' Ramesh Chandra would tell his sons. To any business leader, it's challenging to sustain business growth. Diversification may be an answer to this problem.

Diversification has been increasingly used by corporations as a strategy for adapting to changes in the business environment. It refers to the entry of firms into new markets with new products. The portfolio of most business groups in India consists of many unrelated businesses. The Tata Group, for instance, comprises affiliates operating in a wide range of sectors: automotive, chemicals, communications, consumer products, energy, engineering services, financial services, hospitality, information technology, and steel. Similarly, the Aditya Birla Group comprises fifty-six companies running businesses as diverse as cement, textiles, telecommunications, financial services and retailing. The Bhaskar Group has businesses in textiles, realty, solvent, cement, besides newspaper – print, e-paper, digital app and radio.

> Conglomerates may be regarded as dinosaurs in the western world, but in emerging markets, they have garnered strong growth and account for 30 to 50% of the top 50 companies. One of the major reasons for diversified groups has been the institutional void and government policies. Before liberalisation in early 1990s, the licensing would tend to put a cap on capacities, geographies and industrial sectors. Liaising with government was a key success factor. Enterprises would seek opportunities based on licenses available and their ability to work with the government. This led to companies entering diversified businesses which many times were completely unrelated. With the economy opening in India and other emerging economies, consumerism accelerated the growth is almost all sectors providing opportunities all over. Many MNCs from western economies also started entering looking for faster growth. The local businessmen provide a good landing pad. The fast economic growth led everyone to exploit unprecedented opportunities with double digit growth and speculative returns.

> Movement happened across value chain – both vertically and horizontally and as well as geographically. New businesses in financial sectors, infrastructure and real estate, passenger and cargo transportation, exports and imports led companies to diversify by using their reserves as well as leveraging their assets. Financial institutions opened their gates with products to suit to their requirements.[59]

Starting the solvent plant became an inflection point for Ramesh Chandra. It also opened his vistas in terms of opportunities, strategies and financing. Until then his business ideas were based on the surplus generated by the media business. When he asked Shukla to draw a plan, he was presented with an investment four times more than the surplus. Ramesh Chandra was a little apprehensive, but he still pursued the plan. For the first time, he had to deal with large financial institutions. So far he had not needed to borrow large sums of money. When the bank issued the cheque and Shukla handed it to him, he could not stop himself and said, 'I have never received such a large cheque!' It is this simplicity and honesty that appealed to Shukla, and he agreed to head the project on Ramesh Chandra's request. They had been working together for more than three years and developed a very good mutual understanding. In a way, Ramesh Chandra's interactions with Shukla during

[59]Tarun, Khanna, and Palepu Krishna. 'Why focused strategies may be wrong for emerging markets'. *Harvard Business Review* 75.4 (1997): pp. 41–51.

the solvent project inspired him to think big, which was likely a cornerstone in Daini foray into Rajasthan. "Once I took the reins, Ramesh Chandra left the management to me. He never interfered in the day-to-day workings. We would meet or talk on the phone quite often, but he would only ask if he could do something. We were able to set up a fine factory and a good team, and very soon we became one of the largest companies in the sector," recalls Shukla.

Family run companies that have persisted over generations despite changing conditions strive for operational excellence. Not just that, they are able to skilfully migrate to new value-creating activities and leave redundant activities and practices. They don't become stuck in traditional businesses or outmoded practices. After exhausting growth opportunities in their core business, they diversify into different industries. When they experience their industry maturing and consolidating around them, they decide either to stay and acquire competitors or sell their outflanked business and redeploy assets. Some are able to successfully parry the disruption of technology or regulation. Such adaptations are profoundly informative.

Consider the Cox Enterprises family company, which started in 1898 through the purchase of The Dayton Daily News. The company continued to expand over the next century through media acquisitions. As of 2000, 80% of Cox Enterprises was still focused on newspapers. 'That's terrifying,' said CEO Alex Taylor, a fourth-generation member of the Cox family in a 2015 interview. Through an intense and studied focus on investment in the telecom industry and automobile-related media, Cox Enterprises has since quadrupled in size while the newspaper industry has essentially collapsed. The company has grown to roughly $21 billion in annual revenue today. 'That,' said Taylor, 'is a testament to diversification, innovation, promoting entrepreneurship in our businesses, and allowing people to try new things.'[60]

The opening up of the Indian economy in the 1990s generated multiple opportunities for all businesses. Ramesh Chandra's solvent project had shown that a good plan from an established business can get institutional financing with a smaller contribution from the proposer. Using the surplus generated from media and solvent businesses, he started venturing into other diversified businesses. What followed was a series of business attempts, some of which helped establish the Bhaskar Industry. However, he told his sons to focus on the newspaper business because 'we must never disturb our core business...it is doing very well'. For every other business, he chose someone who was not from the family to lead. This way, he was able to insulate the media business from the risks of diversification and at the same time venture into many businesses, including textile, real estate, cement and power.

---

[60]https://hbr.org/2020/02/what-makes-a-family-business-last

Phase III: The Media House

Investment in core competencies is the source of competitive advantage, say experts. Companies that have invested in becoming lean and flexible in order to respond rapidly to environment and market changes, benchmark continuously to achieve best practice and outsource aggressively to achieve efficiencies. The Japanese are famous for deriving competitive advantage through operational effectiveness. These investments in achieving operational efficiency have resulted in operational improvements and competitive advantage but have failed to secure sustainable advantage. Strategy and operational effectiveness, experts say, are both essential for superior performance, which is the ultimate goal of any enterprise.

Achieving sustained and profitable growth is extremely difficult, and the Bhaskar Group could not have achieved it without having a strong and differentiated core business to build on. Building this strong and differentiated core required access to some form of competitive advantage that the organisation enjoyed and has been able to maintain even after Ramesh Chandra.

Western and Japanese companies have converged on 'similar formidable' standards for product cost and quality. These are more important as qualifying criteria for continued competition and less important as sources of competitive advantage. The real sources of competitive advantage are related to companies' ability to consolidate technologies and production skills into competencies that empower businesses to adapt quickly to changing opportunities. Ramesh Chandra always maintained and also encouraged his sons to remain focused on the core competencies and invest in their development to be successful, and 'de-emphasise activities that do not add value'.

Ramesh Chandra saw to it that the organisation continued to grow. He renewed his focus on innovating his products and services by proactively concentrating on single-business or vertical-diversification strategies. *Dainik Bhaskar's* approach to differentiation strategy, wherein a firm selects one or more attributes that many customers in an industry perceive as important and uniquely positions itself to meet the customers' needs, helped it reach an enviable place in the industry. Thanks to its uniqueness, it has been able to retain a leading position in the market. "He would study the market need and the competitors' strengths and weaknesses to identify the gaps that would have a clear demand for a long time to come, not just in terms of new customers but also its consumption," says Pawan. "This gave him the opportunity to keep innovating based on even small inputs from the customers as well as channel partners, and then he would ask us to create a product or offers that would leap ahead of the current competitive offers. Try the difficult option, he would say and push us to go for it. And we did achieve all of those."

It is because of this uniqueness that the DB group enjoys preferred access to resources or customers' continued loyalty. Ramesh Chandra's grasp over the pulse of the market made the product a strategic fit which could be attained by combining different activities in the firm in order to achieve competitive advantage that is achieved through the way activities of a firm fit and reinforce one another.

> Southwest Airlines' rapid gate turnarounds are essential to its high convenience, low-cost positioning. This it achieves partly through well-paid gate crews, flexible union rules, no meals offered on flights, no seat assignment, no baggage transfer, effective airport selection, strict limits on the type and length of routes and standardized aircraft.[61]

That *Prakash* would spread its light across twelve states in thirty-five years and become the country's leading Hindi daily (*Dainik Bhaskar*) is the stuff dreams are made of. From a four-page newspaper to broadsheet, e-paper, radio (94.3 MY FM) and now digital (DB Digital has six portals and four apps in Hindi, Gujarati, English and Marathi), from treadle machine to world-class German-make KBA printing machines that print 85,000 copies per hour, from a staff comprising few people to thousands of employees, from one newspaper to five newspapers with 65 editions, from few hundred readers to a readership of 6.63 crores, *Prakash* aka *Dainik Bhaskar* has come

---

[61]Rijamampianina, Rasoava, Russell Abratt, and Yumiko February. 'A framework for concentric diversification through sustainable competitive advantage.' *Management Decision* (2003).

a long way in a very short span of time.

Ramesh Chandra and his father Dwarka Prasad were poles apart. While his father was domineering and demanding, Ramesh Chandra was humble and easy going. However, the aggressive businessman in him came alive after he took over the reins of the newspaper following a split from his father in the early 1980s. From that day onwards till he took his last breath, Ramesh Chandra spent his waking hours working, expanding and building his empire. Nothing intimidated him. However crazy an idea was, he would approach it with due diligence and a childlike curiosity. As Elon Musk would put years later, "If you accept all probabilities, that diminishes all fear because the drive overrides fear. When something is important enough, you do it even if the odds are not in your favour. It's all about believing in future and that future would be better than past."

Gordon Moore, co-founder of Intel, demonstrated this quality in the mid-1960s when he proposed what we now refer to as 'Moore's Law'. Moore understood the complexities of the semiconductor industry, its underlying science, and the technical constraints of optical lithography. He was deeply immersed in the details, yet could rise above them – to a place from which he could see more broadly. Moore's knowledge and his vantage point as R&D director of Fairchild Semiconductors led him to predict that the processing power of integrated circuits would

> double every 18 months. That clear, simple insight proved remarkably accurate for more than 30 years and greatly influenced one of the world's most dynamic industries.[62]

"*Dainik Bhaskar* had established itself in Bhopal. But the launch of the Indore edition [in 1983] was the inflection point for Ramesh Chandra," states Shyam Sunder. *Dainik Bhaskar* had organised a fair in Indore, which charged an entry fee. The fair had attracted a lot of visitors, and this did not sit well with the competitors. They complained to the excise department. They also vandalised the fair and informed the police. Even though the police found all the records to be proper and the vandalisers to be outsiders hired to disrupt the event, Ramesh Chandra decided to close the fair. He was agonised and while returning to Bhopal decided that he would launch their Indore edition. He found a land suitable for setting up the press and asked his father for Rs. 5 lakh. His father initially declined as he found it risky. Ramesh Chandra told him that this would be the last time he would ask for any investment from him. His father relented. Ramesh Chandra went deep into the market and met distributors, readers and advertisers. The Indore edition was launched, and very soon it took leadership away from *Nayi Dunia*. This strong resolve and unrelenting obsession with customers had been Ramesh

[62]Keelin, Tom, and Robin Arnold. 'Five habits of highly strategic thinkers: strategic perspective'. *Journal of Business Strategy* 23.5 (2002): pp. 39–44.

Chandra's hallmark in succeeding in almost every business he started. "I consider him a maverick," recalled Shyam Sunder, overcome with emotion as he narrated his fond memories of Ramesh Chandra.

By maintaining a balance between different situations and requirements, Ramesh Chandra expanded his business bit by bit. As a leader with strategic perspective, he could create clarity out of complex and seemingly disconnected details. For instance, he understood the competitive forces shaping his industry, where that industry was headed, and his company's opportunities to succeed, if not dominate. It was as if he was observing the industry and his company simultaneously from the inside and the outside. He could feel the winds of change, sense points of conflict and opportunity, and articulate in concrete and compelling terms how to address them. He could cut to the heart of a problem and was able to generate ideas that were clear and compelling, ideas that others willingly followed. Not all are born with a capacity for strategic perspective. However, chances of improving it over time increase, when one practices these habits:[63]

1. **Get into the game:** Active engagement with difficult issues helped Ramesh Chandra develop strategic perspective. His mind could develop insights on nearly any topic. For instance, focusing on customers' problem would help him gain

[63]Keelin, Tom, and Robin Arnold. 'Five habits of highly strategic thinkers: strategic perspective'. *Journal of Business Strategy* 23.5 (2002): pp. 39–44.

insights on improving his products and services. So, he would identify a problem, focus on it and see where his thoughts led him. Being actively engaged in the game in this way was one of the keys to his strategic perspective.

2. **Embrace confusion and contradictory thoughts:** One of Ramesh Chandra's innate qualities was listening to everyone's ideas no matter how conflicting they were. In doing so he was able to balance what customers wanted with what the company's brightest minds knew was possible. "He understood what happened in the past even as he had his eyes on the future options and prospects," says Sudhir because 'the past is important so far as it affects the future'.
3. **Be calm even amid chaos:** Even amid intense chaos or discussion, Ramesh Chandra would remain calm. It allowed his mind to create space for thoughts so that he could solve problems. He didn't let unimportant issues sap his attention. He took in only good ideas that would add value to his organisation. He believed juxtaposition of contradictory ideas was the root of creativity.
4. **Manage thoughts:** Ramesh Chandra didn't let irrelevant thoughts crowd his mind and concentrated only on those that helped him achieve his goals. He latched onto good ideas as they occurred and didn't let them slip through his fingers.
5. **Cultivate clarity of expression:** He would hear

> all kinds of ideas – good and bad. When it came to expressing his own, he would do it in a way that others benefitted from them. Clarity of thought and vision enabled him to reach out to others and vice versa. Knowing who your customers are and what they want ensures you have their interests and in return your organisation's in focus.

After conquering the Hindi heartland (Madhya Pradesh, Rajasthan), winning the heart of the elite Chandigarh, putting its stamp on Haryana and wrestling a powerful position from the reigning vernacular daily in Gujarat, the Bhaskar Group made a stupendous entry into Mumbai, the financial capital of India, with an English newspaper. It was a high point for the Agarwals, and of course, *Dainik Bhaskar*, which till then was predominantly Hindi. But Ramesh Chandra was a man who took on a challenge head on. With dauntless determination, he laid siege to the Maximum City for maximum gain from one of the world's top centres of commerce. It was the toughest and the biggest challenge so far because he was trying to take on the ruling newspaper, the *Times of India*, that too in the busiest commercial hub of the country. An ideas man and a strategist who knew how to play his cards as per the demands of the time, Ramesh Chandra, for the first time, entered into a partnership with another media baron – Zee TV's Subhash Chandra – and thus *DNA* (*Daily News Analysis*) was born.

DNA was an ambitious project on every scale for the Agarwals, who employed the best in the advertising world and marketing. Pawan took care of the advertisements, while Girish handled marketing. Before the launch, hundreds of hoardings with 'Speak up, it's in your DNA' had sprung up across Mumbai, taking Mumbaikars by surprise. The runup to the launch was very promising, but they were not ready for the surprise that their competitor, *TOI*, threw at them. "None of the competitors in any of our markets ever threw a surprise at us. However, we were caught off guard and suffered a little setback in Mumbai after the *DNA* launch. *TOI* did not surprise us completely but partly. We couldn't react the way we were known to do in our own markets because of various reasons," says Sudhir while reflecting on how Ramesh Chandra was able to recognise a gap in the market and was often able to calculate the risks involved before taking the plunge. However, Mumbai proved a different ball game.

Sudhir explains, "Two things were very clear. Rameshji identified a gap but never made plans on the basis of the weakness of a competitor. That was never the plan, never ever. It was never in his plan to ride on someone else's weakness. Instead, he would say, ride on the market gap. Secondly, he was very clear that one should not build a business by cutting someone else's line short. He would say, 'There's lot of scope in the market and we have to build a very big line.' We followed that practice everywhere. When we were in Rajasthan, *Patrika* was selling four lakh copies and *Navjyoti* maybe seventy to eighty thousand in all of Rajasthan. It was believed to be a five-lakh copy market, but it was actually a thirty-five-lakh copy market.

Patrika used to earn Rs 15 crore. Today, it earns Rs 150 crore. He always believed that 'there's potential in the market, so let's exploit that. Don't exploit the competition, only identify the gap in the market and work on that gap.' He would always look at the bigger picture."

Phase IV: Digital presence

Taking on challenges, tapping into opportunity leads, and entering unchartered territories was in Ramesh Chandra's DNA/genes. When the group decided to venture into radio, their thought process was different because it was a different enterprise. There was no existing player, so there was no competition. They decided to enter only those markets where they were selling their newspapers. The thumb rule was 'don't try and play beyond your strength'. "The fundamental idea was to play to our strengths. Rameshji was very clear that we should not bid for metro cities like Mumbai, Delhi or Kolkata. A lot of people said to bid for Uttar Pradesh and several other places, but he said no. We were very clear that we wanted to play to our strength in our market. That's why Bhaskar acquired licences only in phase 1 and 2, and we are only in those markets where we have our strength in print, brand and network," says Sudhir.

True to his style, Ramesh Chandra launched 94.3 MY FM Radio in Jaipur as a completely independent vertical. As it was the group's first radio station, a core team of Bhaskar was formed to understand the capex and bidding process. There were not many people in the market at the time. A CEO was hired from within the Bhaskar team, and he was moved with the core team to Jaipur. "Being an independent business, it has its own CEO, business head, sales head and finance head. But it has the culture and values of the Bhaskar Group," sums up Sudhir.

The company launched cable network and local channels like Bhaskar TV in Jaipur. However, they closed these businesses as they found these not in line with their way of working. It also launched a monthly Hindi magazine *Aha Zindagi* positioned as a complete family magazine. All these helped Bhaskar to reach a wider reader base. Although the company has operations in oil extraction, hospitality, travel and textile industry, publishing continues to be Bhaskar Group's flagship business.

According to co-founder and CEO of financial services firm Avendus Capital, Gaurav Deepak, "One has to navigate the path around how much ambiguity one can deal with, how much unchartered path one can tread on, how much boldness one has and how much risk one can take. Some manage to organically grow their business. Then there are others who branch out. Some are successful, some are not. When the Bhaskar Group started out, it had roots in a few things in the media in Bhopal. Once their core business (media) became big, they created other multiple businesses. That was value creation. They saw that there was scale on the media side. They could have engaged in digital early on, but as seen globally every traditional media found it difficult to move to digital media. They, however, still branched out. Their way of value creation was taking more risk. I think Mr. Agarwal had that boldness. They were in real estate too and made investments there. And when the chips were down, I didn't see them getting challenged."

It is often argued that for diversification to create value, the firm must keep the relatedness (coherence) of its businesses high. In the words of Benjamin Franklin, "Without continual growth and progress, such words as *improvement*, *achievement* and *success* have no meaning."

5

The Galvaniser

August 2010, Bhopal. The Bhaskar Group launched DB Mall in Bhopal. Ramesh Chandra's goal to provide Bhopal's residents a world-class shopping, theatre and dining experience under one roof finally materialised. With this launch, the group consolidated its position in the real estate sector. DB Infrastructure Pvt. Ltd., its realty arm, got the much-needed boost with the start of the mall, which until then was struggling to make projects such as housing colonies successful. The man who made the mall and other realty projects happen was Ravi Datt Sawla. Ramesh Chandra had handpicked Sawla for the job as he wanted an enterprising individual with a strong understanding of the real estate business to lead the company. Sawla was initially in the accounts department and was selected largely based on his association with Sudhir. He was given a free hand to run the company and was instrumental in turning around the company by introducing a few changes in the housing segment like price for investors and first-time buyers. DB Infrastructure has since then expanded further, especially in tier-I and tier-II cities such as Indore, Gwalior and Bhopal in Madhya Pradesh; Raipur in Chhattisgarh; and Ahmedabad in Gujarat.

What can bees teach business leaders?

"Rameshji would call in the morning and ask a lot of questions but never got into tactical questions like pricing. He trusted me with the job. He had a magnetic personality that would attract people to him just as honeybees are attracted to a hive. Ramesh Chandra envisioned an organisation where everyone would have an obsession with what is good for the whole organisation or team or group and not just for any one person, just like bees. His vision, strategy and belief made us realise that anything is possible. He inspired us to get on board and commit ourselves to the greater purpose and direction," says Sawla.

Leaders can learn so much from honeybees that work with single-minded focus to make a perfect product – honey.[64] Rich in minerals, vitamins, enzymes and water, honey has all the essential matter to sustain life. Just as every single bee is familiar with the honey flow so was Ramesh Chandra immersed in the flow of work. He would rather be present in the moment than observing from a removed position. Leaders like him put themselves at

[64]Avery, Gayle, and Harald Bergsteiner. *Sustainable leadership: Honeybee and locust approaches*. Routledge, 2012.

the centre of the organisation and move freely among the workforce to get the big picture. This enabled him to identify challenges, bottlenecks and constraints and work closely with his people to address them.

To a leader who engages self among equals, neither position nor status matters. What matters is the ability to build and sustain trustful relations with diverse stakeholders, which becomes the key facilitator in building stakeholder social capital. This 'zooming in and out' of different levels of analysis (individuals and social structure) and leader network configurations promise to be a very fruitful approach.[65]

Such leaders are able to display inclusive leadership behaviour. Specifically, pro-diversity beliefs, humility, and cognitive complexity increase the likelihood that individuals will engage in inclusive leadership. Pro-diversity beliefs allow Individuals to hold varying views regarding the benefits and drawbacks of diversity in work groups.[66] Humility creates a self-view that one is "not the center of the universe" in his or her relationships with others. Humble leaders are prone to see the needs of others and understand ways to incorporate others and the unique talents of individuals into the group's functioning because

---

[65]Cullen, Kristin L., Charles J. Palus, and Craig Appaneal. 'Developing Network Perspective Understanding the Basics of Social Networks and their Role in Leadership'. Center for Creative Leadership. Retrieved April 6 (2014): 2020.

[66]Randel, Amy E., et al. 'Inclusive leadership: Realizing positive outcomes through belongingness and being valued for uniqueness'. *Human Resource Management Review* 28.2 (2018): pp. 190–203.

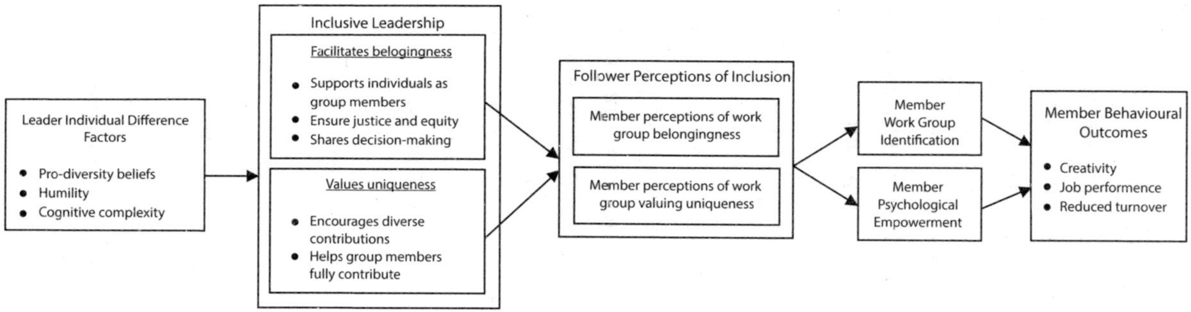

Figure 5.1*

*Randel, Amy E., et al. 'Inclusive leadership: Realizing positive outcomes through belongingness and being valued for uniqueness.' *Human Resource Management Review* 28.2 (2018): pp. 190–203.

of their own self-awareness. Cognitive complexity is an individual's ability to perceive the behaviour and social information of others in a multidimensional manner. Leaders with high levels of cognitive complexity are likely to recognise member strengths even while perceiving limitations rather than applying a one-dimensional view that may minimise member abilities to contribute.

Jud Jao, Ya Jod Lo

'*Jud jao, ya jod lo* – involve everybody,' Ramesh Chandra would always say as he believed that one can be inclusive without losing one's identity. Inclusiveness was his mantra in business as well as in social causes. He galvanised the business and organisations under him. He gave people huge amount of ownership. He used to make them die for what they wanted to do. For instance, if a person who could barely run 10 metres would start running 100 metres after just few weeks with him. What could have brought the change in him? Nothing much, just a little bit of change in that person's approach after spending some time in Ramesh Chandra's company. Such was his pulling power that any person could align with him in seconds; that person could see a win while being with him. "Most importantly, he never took the credit. He never worked to get the credit. People used to feel empowered with him. They said it seemed they had been in a 'jail' before *Dainik Bhaskar* happened to them. He would create a positive atmosphere and tell people they were capable of doing much more and that made them feel empowered," says Pawan.

"This is not a 1996 story. This continued till he was 72, till the day he was alive. The only thing that changed between 1996 and when he was 72 was his increased interest in social organisations and people outside our own organisation. When he passed away, people whom we had never met came to pay tribute to the 'Chairman Sir' who had been actively mentoring them for the past few years," remember both Sudhir and Pawan. A leader who is humble has a better grasp on organisational needs because he knows how to inspire; how to be patient as teams take time to coalesce; how to listen more than command; and, how to provide the vision that sustains momentum while the hard work of family governance is performed.

Seven Reasons to Develop a Network Perspective[67]

1. Connections matter. Individuals do not exist in isolation and their connections provide opportunities (access to value information and resources) and also create constraints. The people they are connected to influence their ideas, attitudes, and behaviours.
2. Work often happens through informal channels. Even after decades of restructuring, work

[67]Cullen, Kristin L., Charles J. Palus, and Craig Appaneal. 'Developing Network Perspective Understanding the Basics of Social Networks and their Role in Leadership'. Center for Creative Leadership. Retrieved April 6 (2014): 2020.

activities often occur through interactions outside of formal reporting and working relationships. Understanding informal networks is especially important in flat, team-based, and agile work environments where formal structure provides little guidance.

3. Leadership occurs through relationships. Direction, alignment, and commitment are created through relationships between people working on shared challenges. All people contribute to this process and thus, leadership may be shared throughout the network. Further, boundary spanning leadership requires network perspective to accurately see and build connections between groups.
4. Successful leaders develop networks of strong, diverse relationships. They realise that under- and over-connectivity stifles performance and limits outcomes. Purposeful (strategic) and authentic networking is the key to developing healthy networks that prevent insularity.
5. Network knowledge is an asset in change efforts. Relying on formal, vertical channels alone hinders capacity to adapt to emerging issues. Change efforts may be accelerated by activating informal networks and enhancing the network's capacity to span boundaries. This approach is critically important in cultural transformation because organisational culture lives largely within the connections between people.

Understanding these connections provides insights into subcultures, pockets of resistance, and hidden champions of the transformation.

6. Innovation networks can be identified and supported. Innovation first requires new, creative ideas. But new ideas are not enough; they must be implemented in the organisation. Research suggests network structures that facilitate creativity and implementation differ from each other in specific ways. Organisations need networks that support the generation and sharing of diverse ideas as well as collective action.
7. The most important challenges leaders face today are it's interconnected. Complex challenges cannot be addressed by individuals alone. They can only be solved by groups of people working collaboratively across boundaries (hierarchies, geographic regions, functional silos, stakeholder interests, and demographic differences). A network perspective is key to thriving in a world in which everything is, or will be, connected.

Inclusive leadership both facilitates belongingness and indicates value for uniqueness in ways that are not fully addressed by other leadership styles. Transformational leadership has a different focus than inclusive leadership in that it relies on the transformation of members to help them "transcend their own immediate self-interest for the sake of the mission and vision of the organisation".

Empowering leadership focuses on facilitating members' control over their own decisions and goals, but does not involve behaviours that facilitate members feeling a sense of belonging within the work group as inclusive leadership does. Inclusive leadership also includes foci that are not fully addressed by servant leadership. Servant leadership has been conceptualised as a leadership style that de-emphasises the self-interests of the leader and instead focuses on the leader's moral responsibility to create success for the organisation, members, and other stakeholders such as customers and the community. Authentic leadership is largely a self-based approach to leadership in that it hinges on the leader being authentic to who he or she is in his or her interactions with others (e.g., "makes decisions based on his/her core beliefs"), rather than focusing on allowing and/or encouraging authenticity in others. Finally, Leader-Member Exchange (LMX) theory explains that leaders form relationships that vary in quality from one member to another.[68]

Like any businessman, Ramesh Chandra wanted to grow his enterprise big and expand beyond the state of Madhya Pradesh. However, he never wanted to achieve triumph by defeating someone or snatching someone's share. No, that was not the game or competition he aspired for. To him "market is big enough for different players, so, let's not step on someone's toes to move ahead'. Even after he established the brand Bhaskar and

[68]Randel, Amy E., et al. 'Inclusive leadership: Realizing positive outcomes through belongingness and being valued for uniqueness'. *Human Resource Management Review* 28.2 (2018): pp. 190–203.

consolidated its position in the market, he adhered to core values that are being practised even today.

No one could remain untouched by his humility. Ramesh Chandra's magic would rub off on anyone who came in contact with him. Even at the pinnacle of his success he remained grounded. That's what makes a true leader who knows his worth and appreciates others' strengths and contribution. The easy manner with which he interacted with others helped them open up to him leading to fruitful discussions. "He was very receptive and would listen to you and your ideas, and if some idea struck him as good he would accept it. He was very open-minded that way. *Jisse bhi baat karte the usi ki tarah ho jate the* (He adapted himself to the times and incorporated people's suggestions.). There used to be discussions for hours before he reached any decision. He would talk to people of any stature with clarity," says Manoj Baheti, who met Ramesh Chandra during the Indore launch in 1982–83 while making a project report for him and became a friend for lifetime.

Importance of values in business success

Once he established any relationship, he would invest in it and manage it well whether it was with his direct reports, peers, superiors, and people outside of the organisation. It helped him obtain supports, resources, and timely information for the group. Research on inter-organisational alliances and networks as well as cross-functional teams also shows that the extent to which leaders are able to

Table 1
Inclusive leadership and other forms of leadership.

Leadership construct	Characteristics	Sample behaviors	Key differences with inclusive leadership
Inclusive leadership	Behaviors that collectively facilitate all group members' perceptions of belongingness to the work group and that encourage group members contributing their uniqueness to achieving positive group outcomes	- Supporting individuals as group members - Ensuring justice and equity within the group - Promoting individuals' diverse contributions to the group - Helping individuals fully provide their unique perspectives, and abilities to the work of the group	N/A
Transformational leadership	Influences members "by broadening and elevating followers' goals and providing them with confidence to perform beyond the expectations specified in the implicit or explicit exchange agreement" (Dvir, Eden, Avolio, & Shamir, 2002: 735).	- Challenging member assumptions - Sharing compelling vision - Developing members - Establishing difficult goals (Bass, 2008; Dvir et al., 2002)	Transformational leadership is focused on motivating and developing members based on the organization's needs while inclusive leadership is focused on accepting members for who they are and allowing them to contribute their unique abilities and perspectives
Empowering leadership	"Behaviors whereby power is shared with subordinates and that raise their level of intrinsic motivation" (Srivastava, Bartol, & Locke, 2006: 1240)	- Leading by example - Teaching how to solve problems - Coaching - Showing that he/she cares (Arnold, Arad, Rhoades, & Drasgow, 2000; Srivastava, Bartol, & Locke, 2006)	Empowering leadership relies on the sharing of power, teaching and coaching, whereas inclusive leadership fosters belongingness and a sense that the individual can contribute based on what makes him or her unique
Servant leadership	Deemphasizes the self-interests of the individual in the leader role and instead is focused on the moral responsibility of the individual to create success for the organization, members, and other stakeholders such as customers, and the community (Ehrhart, 2004; Greenleaf, 1977)	- Behaving ethically - Putting members first - Helping members grow and succeed - Creating value for the community (Liden, Wayne, Zhao, & Henderson, 2008)	Servant leadership focuses on developing and creating success for the members but not necessarily on tending to member needs for work group belonging or uniqueness
Authentic leadership	"Behavior that draws upon and promotes both positive psychological capacities and a positive ethical climate, to foster greater self-awareness, an internalized moral perspective, balanced processing of information, and relational transparency on the part of leaders working with followers, fostering positive self-development" (Walumbwa, Avolio, Gardner, Wernsing, & Peterson, 2008, p. 94)	- Telling members the hard truth - Displaying genuine emotions - Making decisions based on core values - Listening carefully (Walumbwa et al., 2008)	Authentic leadership relies on authentic leader actions and behaviors. In contrast inclusive leadership is focused on ensuring the members experience acceptance and are able to contribute their unique talents and perspectives
Leader-member exchange	Explains that leaders form relationships with members that vary in quality, and that these relationships "reflect the extent to which the leader and subordinate exchange resources and support beyond what is expected based on the formal employment contract" (Liden, Erdogan, Wayne, & Sparrowe, 2006, p 723)	- Helping members know where they stand with him/her - Understanding member problems and needs - Recognizing member potential - Helping member overcome problems (Scandura & Graen, 1984)	LMX is focused on facilitating the positive exchange of resources and support between leaders and members. In contrast, inclusive leadership creates feelings of belongingness and a sense that the individual's ability to contribute his or her uniqueness is valued and welcomed by the organization

accurately diagnose and influence the broader environment affects the performance of their organisation. "*Woh logon se kaam nikalwana jaante the* (He had a knack for getting work done by everyone he came in contact with)," says Sudhir because it is a key quality of a responsible leader to act as weaver and broker of *social capital.* Himanshu Jhavar, who worked with Ramesh Chandra in dealing with financial institutions, concurs with this. "He would meet with bank officers at both the CGM level and the loan officers. In every situation, he sought their advice on how the company's financial requirements could be met in the best possible manner, rather than simply demanding a loan. This approach built a strong emotional bond with all our bankers. Anyone from the Bhaskar Group was always welcome because we never defaulted on loan repayments, nor did we ever exceed our overdraft limits," adds Himanshu.

Investing in social capital

A visionary like Ramesh Chandra moves people towards shared dreams. He helped people see how their work fit into the big picture. If people got the feeling that their work mattered, then they also understood why. To articulate a truly inspirational vision, he was able to sense how others felt and understood their perspectives. Many a time, this proved effective in bringing about a turnaround.

Ramesh Chandra invested in people with a long-term, internally focused view. He created a sense of social mission that is served when the business succeeded. He aimed at achieving a high level of employee engagement and openness. He was able to strike a beautiful balance between focus on culture and human capital, and the strategy function, setting the agenda and taking a visible role in shaping the strategies his team would develop. He was able to combine a structural planning and analysis while creating incentives, organisational structures, and culture that enabled an improvisational approach to strategy. For him a strategy was a set of enduring general principles for competing, such as developing competencies, embracing social purpose, and taking the long view, an approach to business that he would personally encode in the company's culture. This not only enhanced agility in the marketplace but also allowed to develop senior managers. For him, strategy and "guiding and teaching" were complementary priorities.

Unlike the feel-good statements that Western companies make about, say, improving customers' lives, the social missions of most Indian companies are integral to their strategy and often the route to profits. A case in point: The hospital group Narayana Hrudayalaya was founded by Devi Shetty to help the thousands of Indian children who need cardiac surgery but can't afford it. The group soon discovered that the only way to provide quality operations cheaply was to standardise them, so it set about learning to perform them at scale. It now performs more than twice as many cardiac surgeries as the biggest U.S. hospital, with outcomes at least as good and at about one-tenth the cost, and its profit margins are slightly above those of its U.S. peers. Other Indian companies similarly interweave strategy and social mission. The telecommunications provider Bharti Airtel sees its mission as getting cell phones into the hands of the hundreds of millions of people in India who otherwise have no way to communicate with one another. Max India's new insurance product, Max Vijay, combines life insurance with savings in a model that allows people with erratic incomes to pay whatever they can, whenever they can. IT companies such as Cognizant and Infosys describe their social mission in part as showing the world that India and Indian companies can compete and win on the international stage.[69]

With his sons taking up responsibility of running the newspaper business, his focus shifted to social causes. Here, too, his involvement was as intense as it was in business matters. He loved to work with youngsters. He would urge 25-year-olds to come and talk to him and would give them responsibilities. He encouraged youth in everything that they did. In fact, he made that a culture – to encourage youth – in associations. 'They have lot of energy, lot of ideas, interact with them, and give them

[69]https://hbr.org/2010/03/leadership-lessons-from-india

responsibilities. Share your experience with them and let them ideate and take that to readers because if I am 60 and I need to understand 20-year-olds then I will have to interact with them,' he would say. "He never used to limit the purpose of any organisation, which also stemmed from the fact that he needed to connect with the ground in those organisations where the majority of working people were 50 and above. He used to say 'sabko jodo ya logon se jud jao'," sums up Pawan.

The magnetic appeal

Did Ramesh Chandra select people or people selected him? It worked both ways. In Ramesh Chandra's case, as the media man he had perspective of network and understanding of the dynamic web of connections that impacted his work and culture of his organisation. He could recognize patterns of relationships and people – both strong and weak ties – in his network, those who would foster strategic success or undermine it.

The establishment of soybean processing plants marked a significant milestone for the Bhaskar Group, marking Ramesh Chandra's first step toward realising his long-cherished dream of becoming an industrialist. After gaining a strong foothold in the media sector, Ramesh Chandra had begun to feel restless for expansion. He scouted for an opportunity to set up a unit in sectors like textiles and sugar. He met several people and made several attempts. It was during this period that he met NM Shukla. He spent hours with Shukla, who showed him the big picture outside media. He told Ramesh Chandra, "If you want to become big, you will have to become an industrialist." It ignited the fire in Ramesh Chandra's belly and he asked Shukla to join him. If Ramesh Chandra saw an able and equally enthusiastic partner in him, Shukla saw an opportunity to grow beyond Eicher where he was at that time. Thus began a partnership, a bond that laid the foundation of the Bhaskar Industry.

Knowing who, when, and how to coordinate is a function of the manager's network of contacts within and beyond the firm.[70] "Since he had the knack for smelling an opportunity, he could easily see one coming his way and tell us or anyone he was interacting with at that point 'if you can do it, then you should'. He loved to work with people who could tap into business opportunity leads and worked on them. He loved to see people becoming successful. He knew more about my friends' businesses and professions than I did. My friends would go to him and talk to him openly than they did with me," remembers Pawan. It was this trait of responsible leadership that enabled him to broker sustainable, mutual beneficial relationships with stakeholders, to create stakeholder goodwill and trust and ultimately a trusted business in society.

According to Madhu Kela, founder at MK Ventures, it was Ramesh Chandra's affable and agreeable disposition that rubbed off on those around him. Kela met him in

[70]Burt, R. S. 'The Contingent Value of Social Capital'. *Administrative Science Quarterly* Vol. 42, pp. 339–365 (1997).

2001 and would address him as 'Bhai saab' though he considered him as father figure. They would discuss stock market and Kela would answer all his queries, which would be numerous, regarding the stock market. They hit it off so well that whenever he was in Mumbai he would try to meet Kela, who remembers him as a genuine, frank and honest person. On his advice, Ramesh Chandra bought his first share – Jindal Steel & Power. He was a true Marwari as business was in his blood. At the same time, he was a down-to-earth and accessible person. "I was one of the very few privileged people with whom he had wine if we met in the evening," Kela fondly recollects the time spent with Ramesh Chandra. His rustic intelligence was endearing because he would demand explanation in very simple language to his simple and straightforward questions like 'how will this business work and how much money will I make'. He had this uncanny ability to understand business in a very raw format and he could smell money. It was during such interactions that the idea of making *Dainik Bhaskar* public clicked to him. Like a true entrepreneur, he thrived on challenges. The more challenging a project, the more fun it was for him to do it. He became ambitious with each success. However, what gave him happiness were both the journey and the destination, says Kela.

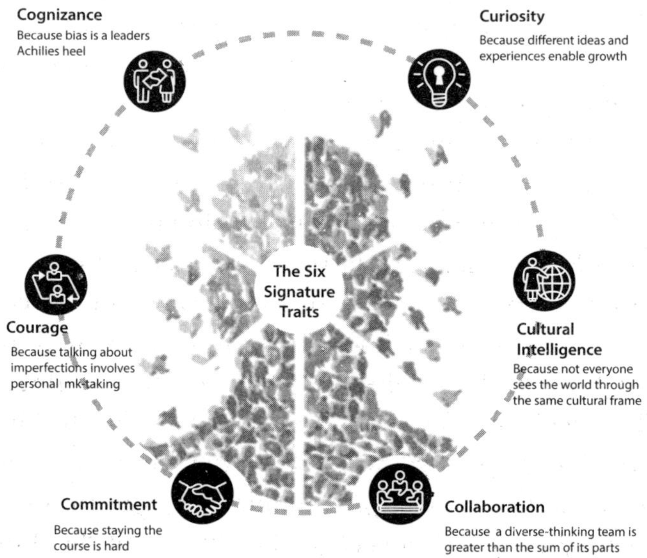

Figure 5.2 The Six Sigma traits of an inclusive leader

Six Signature Traits of an Inclusive Leader[71]

- Committed to diversity and inclusion because these objectives align with their personal values and because they believe in the business case.
- Able to speak up and challenge the status quo, and they are humble about their strengths and weaknesses.

[71]https://www2.deloitte.com/us/en/insights/topics/talent/six-signature-traits-of-inclusive-leadership.html

- Mindful of personal and organisational blind spots, and self-regulate to help ensure "fair play".
- Open minded with a desire to understand how others view and experience the world, and have a tolerance for ambiguity.
- Confident and effective in cross-cultural interactions.
- Able to empower individuals as well as create and leverage the thinking of diverse groups.

Impact of emotional intelligence

Leaders set the emotional standard of the organisation. A leader's moods and emotions send strong signals across the organisation. Negative emotions not only erode our mental abilities but also make people emotionally less intelligent. A person who is upset finds it difficult to be empathic as he has trouble in reading the emotions of others around them. On the other hand, positive emotions bring out the best in people. It was the optimistic outlook of Ramesh Chandra that often helped him reach his goal. "He would never show his emotions in discussions. Nobody who has met him has ever found him disturbed, angry or agitated. His composed posture would always put us at peace and made us think innovatively. His leadership was so resonant that people were often pulled to him and they felt upbeat and enthusiastic, and vibrated with their leader. Working with him brought out the best in them. Resonance amplified the emotional impact of his leadership", Shyam Sunder claims. Emotional Intelligence has four components:[72]

a. **Self-awareness:** This means having a deep understanding of one's strengths, limitations, values and motives. Ramesh Chandra had self-awareness and was honest with himself about himself. Research says self-reflection and thoughtfulness are two common attributes found in people like him as they reflect things over and do not react impulsively.

b. **Self-management:** This covers attributes like emotional self-control, transparency, adaptability, achievement, initiative and optimism. Even in precarious situations, Ramesh Chandra never wavered. He could control his feelings, facilitate mental clarity and provide controlled energy. *DNA* was his most ambitious project as he was entering into a fiercely competitive terrain – English newspaper market – in India's commercial capital, Mumbai. Though he started on a good note, it didn't click. He didn't lose sleep over it as it was not in his *DNA* to linger over loss. He simply moved on sending a message to all that 'there are other battles to win'.

c. **Social awareness:** This includes empathy, organisational awareness and ability to serve client/customer needs. Being attuned to how others feel, Ramesh Chandra could say and do what

[72]https://online.hbs.edu/blog/post/emotional-intelligence-in-leadership

was appropriate, to calm fears, assuage anger or join in good spirits. Easy approachability, ability to listen and responding suitably were something that came naturally to him. He won over people as empathy is often the key to retaining talent.

d. **Relationship management:** This involves influencing and developing others, change management, conflict management, building bonds and teamwork. As a true captain of the ship, he steered people in the right direction.

A group's emotional intelligence requires the same capabilities that an emotionally intelligent individual expresses.[73] Groups have moods and needs and they act collectively in the group. Leaders must understand how they are feeling and be alert for important signals. Emotionally intelligent leaders are good at managing their disruptive emotions. They keep their focus, thinking clearly under pressure. They are prepared to change before a crisis. Even during tumultuous times, they can visualise a brighter future, communicate that vision with resonance and lead the way. They create a climate of enthusiasm and flexibility where people feel most innovative and give their best.

Leaders who practice both leading outward and leading inward can boost employee experiences of being valued, authentic, trusted, and psychologically safe at

[73]https://hbr.org/2001/03/building-the-emotional-intelligence-of-groups

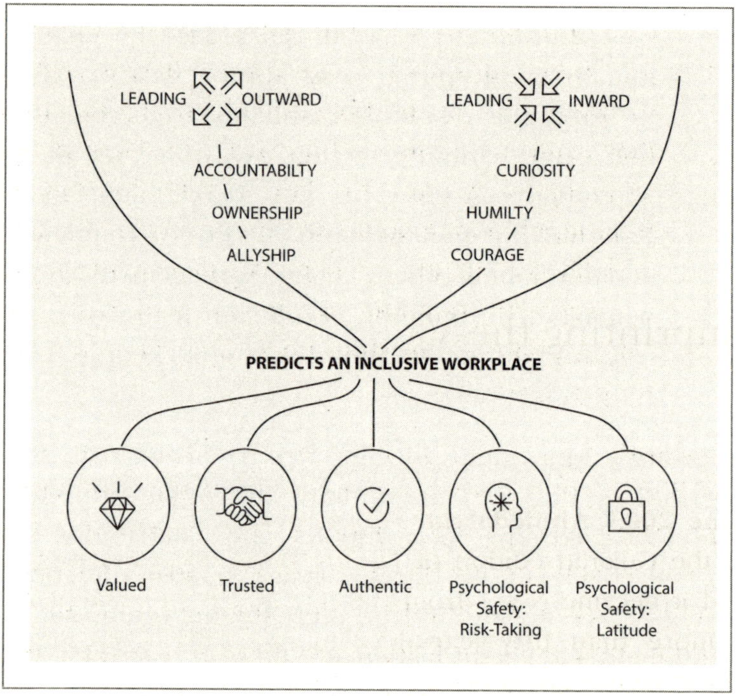

Figure 5.3 Leading Outward & Leading Inward

work – the hallmarks of an inclusive workplace.[74] These experiences benefit employees and companies in tangible ways – increasing team problem-solving, employee engagement, retention, and employee innovation. Leading outward is what you do to ensure team members are treated fairly, empowered, and able to flourish. Leading inward requires a hard look at who you are and your inner ability to act courageously, learn, and self-reflect.

[74]https://www.catalyst.org/wp-content/uploads/2020/03/Getting-Real-About-Inclusive-Leadership-Report-2020update.pdf

6

Imprinting the Value Codes

June 2003, Ahmedabad. *Divya Bhaskar* (the name given to the Gujarati edition of *Dainik Bhaskar*), was launched and it became No. 1 from the day of its launch replacing a more than fifty-year-old Gujarati daily. The group's objective has always been to build a strong and loyal base of readers. Information driven marketing systems, developed on a foundation of extensive research, were central to its strategy. Such a system always helped shift the focus of the organisation from mere circulation to individual readers. "Experience has taught us that a good product generates new readers," says Sudhir echoing his father's concerns.

The readers were central to Ramesh Chandra's endeavours. He believed that readers had every right to know the truth, and he aimed to tell them that through his newspaper. Even in other ventures, his outward-looking strategy eventually helped him achieve personal and group goals. 'Times change and circumstances change, but one should never change one's values,' he would say. Just as any family firm is endowed with a bundle of beliefs and practices that constitute their tradition, the Bhaskar Group has its core values and behavioural attributes put down on paper. "We want to have an understanding with the person we are hiring whether he fits into the culture – we check his family background, his way of conducting himself, his past work – that's how we know whether he has culture fitment or not. We hire people who can align with our culture. If you don't align with our culture, we can't change ours for you. We can change processes, systems, which is important to run and grow the business, but we can't change the value and culture of the company," says Sudhir, who understands that to remain competitive they need to renew and update their products without compromising on the firm's core values.

During the promotion of the 'Think Different' campaign in 1997, Apple CEO Steve Jobs' iconic speech went on to become one of the best marketing strategies. He said people with passion can change the world for the better. To him marketing was about values. So, in its brand marketing campaign Apple went back to its core value. "The marketing is in a totally different world from where it was a decade ago. And Apple is totally different and Apple's place in it is totally different. The products, the distribution strategy and the manufacturing are totally different. We understand that. But values and core values shouldn't change. The things that Apple believed in at its core are the same things Apple really stands for today,' said the tech trailblazer. He wanted to find a way to communicate this and what he helped create moved many as the campaign honoured those people who have changed the world.[75]

While Apple was making waves in the Western tech world with its innovative products, India saw the emergence of a Hindi newspaper in one of its central states, riding the wave of economic liberalisation. The broadsheet, *Dainik Bhaskar*, was born in 1983 in Indore, Madhya Pradesh, though it was founded in 1958 by Ramesh Chandra's father Dwarka Prasad. Today, the Dainik Bhaskar group is present in 13 states with 65 editions in Hindi, Marathi and Gujarati. Just as Apple stood for revolution and change, the Bhaskar brand brought a new and fresh perspective, and changed people's mindset about Hindi or local language newspaper. It gave the Hindi daily an image makeover.

People, for the first time, began associating with Hindi newspapers. The success fuelled Ramesh Chandra's ambition, and he began leaving a trail of conquests in the media world. Driven by passion and purpose, the revolutionary media baron used both old and new tricks to scale up his business. The master builder combined the wisdom he gained working with his father with

[75]Walter Isaacson, Steve Jobs, Simon & Schuster, 2011.

techniques available in the new world. He was quite adept at blending the old and the new.

Research, marketing and core values

Research has been integral to the group's marketing efforts. Targeted surveys yielded favourable results for all their launches across India. Girish made it clear at the outset that the launch of *Divya Bhaskar* in Ahmedabad would be a bigger version of any marketing efforts by the company so far. He reinforced that, like other previous efforts, this launch would also pre-market the paper and get confirmed paid-up circulation. The readers would know in advance that a new newspaper was being published, and they would tell the hawkers to deliver the paper to their doorsteps on a given date. The marketing efforts involved the people of Gujarat to make a newspaper for and by them, thus reinforcing the latent need for a good and different newspaper. It was understood within the Bhaskar Group that the campaign would be turned around in as short a period as possible to converge all the market attention in a limited span and to minimise the competition response time. It was going to be a game of speed, precision and logistics management.

It was decided that *Divya Bhaskar* would be launched at Ahmedabad followed by other cities – Surat, Vadodara and then Rajkot – depending upon the extent of success. Ahmedabad would be able to cater to most of northern Gujarat, while Surat would take care of the southern part, till a full-fledged expansion was brought about. The launch plan had three phases. The first phase involved research that primarily identified readers' expectations, in terms of content and spread. It also identified areas of discontent with existing newspapers. The research had another initial objective: to create awareness about *Divya Bhaskar* among the readers of other newspapers before the launch of the edition. In the second phase, a mass media campaign was launched. In the third phase, order booking was carried out. Thus, the customers were contacted twice: first during the need identification survey and secondly at the time of booking orders.

Managing tradition and innovation

In family firms, tradition is handed down from generation to generation, for example, through storytelling, physical objects embodying values, and rituals. It implies the strong recognition of ancestors who imprinted the 'organisational tradition' at the formation stage, which survives and persists over time, within and among generations.[76] The invariant core of tradition shapes the family firm's identity and its modus operandi, paving the way for continuity, and spurring next generations to accept and enact it. Thus, shared beliefs, rituals, practices, and legacy help family firms persist over time, albeit potentially posing a

[76]Erdogan, Irmak, Emanuela Rondi, and Alfredo De Massis. 'Managing the tradition and innovation paradox in family firms: A family imprinting perspective'. *Entrepreneurship theory and practice* 44.1 (2020): pp. 20–54.

substantial constraint to change, particularly for those with high attachment to their tradition. Nevertheless, family firms need to change and innovate to remain competitive.

Ramesh Chandra's family played a unique role in the building of his empire as it mattered the most to him. It was and still is a close-knit family that has stuck together through thick and thin, through successes and failures, through the most difficult times and the happiest times. The family has proactively kept the concept of togetherness alive. While dealing with crisis situations, Ramesh Chandra and his sons have always been on the same page. Such bonhomie and understanding among members are rarely seen in big, joint families. If he had been able to forge ahead with single-mindedness, then the credit goes to the support he enjoyed from his wife and children. His wife stood by his side like a pillar of strength bearing all the burden of taking care of the family and raising their kids, who were very small when he started out on his own (after he left his father's home following a rift) from an old building that housed the newspaper office on the ground floor while his family stayed on the upper floor in a hall-like room. His early days of struggle after he left his father's house with his wife and children, and the values that he passed on to them have made them cherish the fact that the family needs to stick together. It was with this understanding that the entire family would shift and settle down in a different city before every launch.

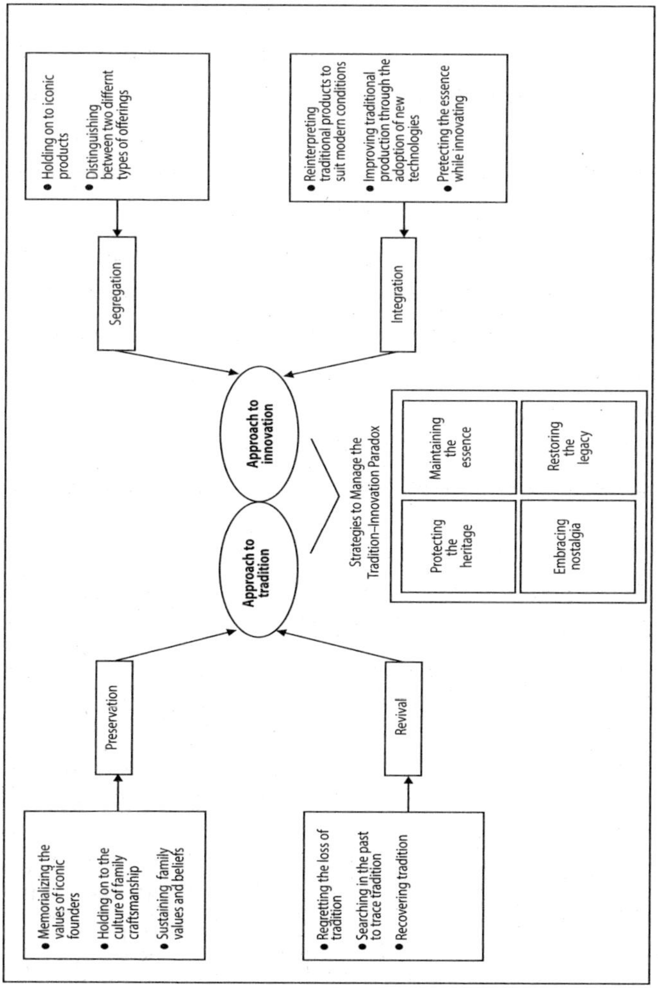

Figure 6.1 Managing Traditions: A Framework[77]

[77]Erdogan, Irmak, Emanuela Rondi, and Alfredo De Massis. 'Managing the tradition and innovation paradox in family firms: A family imprinting perspective'. *Entrepreneurship theory and practice* 44.1 (2020): pp. 20–54.

"It was about commitment, which means wholeheartedly dedicating yourself to a task without distraction. When we launched editions in different cities, our commitment extended beyond just work. The entire family relocated to each new place. Being physically present had two significant benefits: first, it allowed us to spend 80 to 90 per cent of our time there; second, it created a moral obligation. When your team operates at ground zero, remote control isn't enough—you need to be there to provide unwavering support and handle unforeseen challenges, he would say," remembers Pawan.

Resilience vs performance

Research shows family businesses focus on resilience more than performance. They forgo the excess returns available during good times in order to increase their odds of survival during bad times. A CEO of a family controlled firm may have financial incentives similar to those of chief executives of non-family firms, but the familial obligation he or she feels will lead to very different strategic choices. Executives of family businesses often invest with a ten or twenty-year horizon, concentrating on what they can do now to benefit the next generation. They also tend to manage their downside more than their upside, in contrast with most CEOs, who try to make their mark through outperformance.[78]

[78]Nicholas Kachenar, George Stalk and Alain Bloch, 'Learning from Family Business', *Harvard Business Review*, November 2012.

Being frugal in good times and bad times

While countless corporations use stock grants and options to turn managers into shareholders and minimise the classic principal–agent conflict, family firms seem imbued with the sense that the company's money is the family's money, and as a result they simply do a better job of keeping their expenses under control. A look at company finances over the last economic cycle shows that family run enterprises entered the recession with leaner cost structures, and consequently they were less likely to have to do major layoffs. Only one-third (34 per cent) of surveyed businesses have had to cut dividends, and 31 per cent of family members have taken salary cuts. Overall, only one in five businesses (21 per cent) needed to access extra capital; 15 per cent of the owners are putting in more of their own cash, and a further 23 per cent say they are prepared to do so if necessary.[79] "Ramesh Chandra was a big risk-taker but he would take risk only with the money he had earned. When we entered Jaipur, our planning was rooted in the company's annual surplus. All our diversification efforts hinged on using the surplus generated by one business to fund other ventures. Additionally, we judiciously supplemented our financial resources with long-term loans, adhering to strict financial prudence and discipline," says P.G. Mishra.

[79]https://www.pwc.com/gx/en/family-business-services/family-business-survey-2021/pwc-family-business-survey-2021.pdf

Keeping the bar high for capital expenditures

Family controlled firms are especially judicious when it comes to capital expenditure (capex). Ramesh Chandra had a simple rule. He did not spend more than he earned. He would be interested in capex investments or building industry only if a project provided a good return on its own merits. He would judge it against other potential projects to keep spending under the company's self-imposed limit. Because they're more stringent, family businesses tend to invest only in very strong projects. "We had entered the oil extraction business and had grown to seven plants. The business was doing fine. However, due to exchange fluctuations and some changes in the regulations, the profitability was being affected and the business was becoming speculative. Ramesh Chandra visited all the plants and met the senior people. As soon as he came back, we were told that we should plan an exit. We presented different scenarios. He had only one question regarding how much we would lose by selling the plants as compared to carrying the business with uncertainty. Almost immediately he decided to close the units rather than play the game speculatively," recalls Himanshu Jhavar.

Carrying little debt

In modern corporate finance a judicious amount of debt is considered a good thing because financial leverage maximises value creation. Family controlled firms, however, associate debt with fragility and risk. Debt means having less room to manoeuvre when a setback occurs and being beholden to a non-family investor. "We would get transfer funds from one company to other but would not approach the banks for loans beyond the limits. It was also possible because most of our businesses generated cash and did not have long receivable cycles," points Himanshu. Ramesh Chandra believed in debt or leveraging, but he never allowed using debt or leverage for cash flows.

Acquire fewer and smaller companies

Of all the plays a manager can make, a sparkly transformational acquisition may be the hardest to resist. It carries high risks but can pay large rewards. Many family businesses eschew these deals. They favour smaller acquisitions close to the core of their existing business or deals that involve simple geographic expansion. However, there are significant exceptions to this rule. Ramesh Chandra, the visionary that he was, never hesitated to dive headfirst into new projects. His conviction stemmed from recognising structural changes or disruptions in traditional sectors. Whenever he sensed that abstaining from industry consolidation could jeopardise the firm's long-term survival, he sprang into action. He favoured greenfield projects over acquiring existing companies, even after encountering setbacks in mining and textile ventures.

Showing surprising level of diversification

Plenty of family controlled companies – such as Michelin and Walmart – remain focused on a core business. But despite a generation's worth of financial wisdom that diversification is better done by individual investors than at a corporate level, a large number of family businesses – such as Cargill, Koch Industries, Tata, and LG – are far more diversified than the average corporation.

Bhaskar Group has expanded into new lines of business organically while others have acquired small entities in new fields and built on them. According to them, as recessions have become deeper and more frequent, diversification has become a key way to protect the family wealth. If one sector suffers a downturn, businesses in other sectors can generate funds that allow a company to invest for the future while its competitors are pulling back. Ramesh Chandra was very careful in choosing the sector and businesses largely based on cash flows, regular customer demand and less burden of account receivables.

Retaining talent better than their competitors

The leaders of family companies extol the benefits of longer employee tenures: higher trust, familiarity with co-workers' behaviours and decision-making, a stronger culture. These businesses have a lot in common with what the academicians Karlene Roberts and Karl Weick call 'high-reliability organisations', in which long-serving teams of specialists develop efficient team dynamics and a collective mind-set that helps them achieve goals.

Interestingly, family businesses generally don't rely on financial incentives to increase retention. Instead, they focus on creating a culture of commitment and purpose, avoiding layoffs during downturns, promoting from within, and investing in people. As Sudhir says, "Acumen is crucial. Passion and cultural fit are equally important. Without passion and alignment with the organisational culture, even the sharpest acumen won't be able to perform. Think of acumen as the key that unlocks the door to business success—you can't run a business without it. Culture fit and genuine enthusiasm are like the well-oiled gears that keep that business engine running smoothly."

Importance of family values

Deeply ingrained family values set the Agarwals apart. This enduring familial bond is formed when parents actively collaborate with their children, nurturing a shared vision and commitment. They create a family culture that transcends the ever-fluctuating world of business, where markets swing from good to bad and sometimes downright tough. But there's one constant: family. This can only come through parental leadership, values or thought process and how they inculcate it. "For the Agarwals, the family has always been in sync with what is happening and they have been with each other at all times. I can see where it is all coming from – Mr. Agarwal's values and the perspective of what is important in life. As a father you put forward what is important in life and life flows that way," says Gaurav Deepak.

He remembers meeting Ramesh Chandra during his periodic visits to Mumbai for brief chats. "It was so nice of him to call me and say 'let's catch up for forty-five minutes'. During those interactions I found him having a wide variety of interests and not limited to media. He had a deep sense of current business and market knowledge. Secondly, his mind was very quick. He was not a wavering guy but a decisive man."

"I have interacted with the family, which has three brothers who are on equal footing. What has struck me is the family value system and how they conduct themselves. I would say only 10 to 15 per cent of the business houses have the level of collaboration and understanding of each other that these three guys have. There has to be an implicit trust and respect for each other for this kind of thing to happen because what you do impacts everyone. There was a collective call among Mr Agarwal, Sudhir and Girish on capital matters as to how much debt or leverage one could take. There was deep collaboration and respect for each other. I think they were also aligned along the path. There was no disjointed view on the path forward. If I were to talk to Sudhir or Girish, I would typically hear the same thing," says Gaurav, who believes that value creation, market share and scale are all linked to each other in the family value creation process. "Growth is the biggest galvaniser of the family. Ramesh Chandra had taken it upon himself to ensure this," adds Shyam Sunder.

> Mario Preve, Chairman of Riso Gallo, an Italian rice producer since 1845, says: "The family business has the advantage that it is not only a matter of profit; it's like your home. I always say that it's like the relay race: someone passes you the baton and then you pass it on to someone else. We say that we didn't get the company from my parents; we are borrowing it from our children. And this is important. We are thinking of how it affects our offspring. We don't think in quarters, we think in generations."[80]

Keeping it in the family

Ramesh Chandra was very clear that the most important thing for a family-owned business is continuity. He was fifteen years old when he was inducted into the family business of a daily newspaper run by his father. It wasn't handed to him on a platter though. His father made sure that he learnt the ropes of the business and rose through the ranks. It helped Ramesh Chandra get firsthand experience in selling newspapers. Later, his father introduced his first grandson, Sudhir, to the newspaper business at a very early age of thirteen. Sudhir joined

[80]https://www.fambiz.com.au/wp-content/uploads/FBN-Ernst-Young-Built_to_Last-FB-Survey.pdf

the business as an office peon and would be at his work place at 4.00 a.m. every day. Girish, the second son, then followed when he was around fifteen years old. The third son, Pawan, was encouraged to study and was sent abroad to gain a technical degree, which he later utilised during the launch of the Jaipur edition. However, Ramesh Chandra never encouraged his only daughter to study or take interest in the business. In fact, none of his daughters-in-law is in any way involved in the business. His sons, though, are open-minded in providing education to their daughters. Sudhir's daughter Shubh has studied abroad and joined the family business at the age of 25. She is very clear about her role in the business. Armed with a degree in business administration and information technology, her first assignment was to develop a content-based app for the group, and she was quite excited about it.

Is it a coincidence that the third generation of the Agarwals has taken a plunge into the family business through the digital route? *Dainik Bhaskar*, like many other media organisations, found itself at a crossroads during the pandemic. It realised that to weather the storm brought upon the global economy by Covid-19, it had to embrace digital transformation. Whichever the case may be, it's been a win-win for the group. First, the interest shown by the third generation in the family-owned business. Secondly, their entry at a time when the industry reeled under pandemic-induced challenges. Young and full of new ideas, they are equipped with the relevant knowledge needed for the group in the ever-evolving digital world.

Strategic education tends to bring the latest knowledge to the firm for the purpose of capitalising on emerging entrepreneurial opportunities. Work experience is similarly used to expose their children to latest practices.[81] Though Sudhir and Girish were not encouraged to get formal education, Pawan was sent abroad to study and encouraged to use his education during the Jaipur launch. Likewise, Shubh is playing an active role in the company's digital project.

As per PwC's India Family Business Survey, more businesses feel vulnerable to digital now. This is perhaps attributable to greater awareness among family business owners and leaders about the avenues going digital can open for companies, and about how by not being a part of the digital revolution, their businesses can get left behind. The survey after discussions with owners and the next generation found out that more and more companies are speaking the digital language as they introduce new models in selling, buying, inventorising and marketing.[82]

"Had Baba been here he would have told us to go digital because he believed in keeping in step with the times. "'Evolve' he would say," says Shubh, who remembers her grandfather as a great visionary; extremely humble

---

[81]Shane, S., Venkataraman, S., 2000. 'The promise of entrepreneurship as a field of research'. *Academy of Management Review* 25, pp. 217–226.
[82]https://www.pwc.in/assets/pdfs/research-insights/fbs/2019/pwc-india-family-business-survey-2019.pdf

with no airs about him and who treated everyone alike. He was progressive because he believed that it was important to change with the times. She fondly reminisces how he gave his nod to using onion and garlic in their food after visiting her in Singapore, where she was studying and had taken a liking to the herbs. He was social as he was very good at talking to people at various levels; a risk-taker who went on to launch successful ventures barring few failures; adjusting and adaptive. Aggressive? "No, not at all." Did he have ambition? "Yes." Passionate? "Yes." She compares her Baba to Dhoni, the cricketing maestro. "Like Dhoni, Baba was a strategist and a finisher," adds Shubh.

Transgenerational business

Literature on transgenerational businesses suggests that 50 per cent of the organisations do not survive beyond the second generation and only 13 per cent survive beyond the third generation.[83] On the other hand, there are organisations that have been running since 1,000 years. Kabushiki Gaisha Kong¯o Gumi, a Japanese construction company, is a continuously ongoing independent company and is currently the oldest known extant company overall, operating for over 1,400 years. There are a lot of European companies that have survived three or five generations. In India, the Wadias are considered the oldest Indian

[83]https://www.johnson.cornell.edu/smith-family-business-initiative-at-cornell/resources/family-business-facts/

family managed company that has been in operation for the last 160 years without changing its vision in these many years.[84]

Legacy is a much bigger term than just passing on the wealth and finances to the next generation. It involves cascading of values, codes, governance mechanisms, family constitutions, conflict resolution mechanism and philanthropy.[85] In case of first-generation businesses, the corporation is managed under the leadership of one person. Also, till it is a public listed company, there is one person in charge. As the next generation comes in, responsibilities, resources as well as authorities are shared. The next generation is a new-world creature, differently educated and with a wider worldview. This may create differences of opinion, working styles, and approaches to professionalism. In many cases, the new generation members are specialists as compared to the founder, who tends to be generalist or at best a technocrat. They do not have to struggle for survival or basic needs of life. Such generation gaps create hurdles and many corporations have suffered. The continuity of values, and their meanings and inculcation pose challenges for many first-generation entrepreneurs.

Theory suggests that environmental influences that occur when one is young remain imprinted in adulthood. Thus, family firms have unique opportunities to imprint beliefs

---

[84]https://en.wikipedia.org/wiki/List_of_oldest_companies

[85]Barnes, Louis B., and Simon A. Hershon. 'Transferring power in the family business'. *Harvard Business Review* 54.4 (1976): pp. 105–114.

and behaviours onto the next generation.[86] Accordingly, childhood involvement in the family firm offers a platform for imprinting the family's entrepreneurial legacy.[87] Both Ramesh Chandra and his eldest son, Sudhir, were inducted very early in life into the family business by his father, Dwarka Prasad. They had seen their respective fathers work at close quarters and imbibed the hard-working and relentless spirit from them.

Childhood interaction with multiple generations provides repeated opportunity for senior family members to share narratives that reconstruct the family's past entrepreneurial acts or resilience. Since Marwadi (business class) families are usually large and live together, the family and firm are one rather than two entities. The next generation, thus, gets involved and hears and learns rhetorical narratives about the entrepreneurial history of the family and firm. Sudhir reminisces how his grandfather impacted his life. He was a headstrong, arrogant and aggressive man while his father was the opposite. Despite their stark differences, his father truly found his calling when he made the decision to launch *Dainik Bhaskar* as a broadsheet from Indore, he remembers.

Shubh remembers her grandfather as a hard-working man who would always say 'trust your gut'. He was a leader who was humble and had a good grasp on organisational needs because he knew how to inspire;

---

[86]https://home.kpmg/dp/en/home/insights/2021/01/the-family-legacy.html
[87]Marquis, C., Tilcsik, A., 2013. *Imprinting: toward a multilevel theory*. Academy of Management Annals, 7, pp. 195–245.

how to be patient as teams take time to coalesce; how to listen rather than command; and, how to provide the vision that sustains momentum while the hard work of family governance is performed.

Roles and involvement

The right levels of involvement based on expertise and interest is essential. Leadership principles and roles should be proactively defined. Two Indian families that have managed the transition well are the Daburs and the Murugappa Group of EID Parry fame. The Dabur family business was founded in 1884 and is one of India's leading FMCG companies (and the world's largest Ayurvedic and natural healthcare companies). The founding family is now in its fifth generation. They also have a family constitution that provides clarity on what roles everyone should play. They hired professional consultants for advice and now have a family council that serves as a forum in which family members broadly have a say in where the group is headed strategically.[88]

The Murugappa Group, for instance, has a group corporate board that has only five family members and each firm is managed by professionals. Each family member retires at sixty-five, they are rotated amongst each firm (to prevent the feeling that one part of the family has

[88]Sanket V. Ravan, 'Family Business Governance System of Dabur Group a Case Study'. *International Journal of Trend in Scientific Research and Development* (IJTSRD), Conference Issue, March 2019.

Figure 6.2 Value Imprinting Framework*

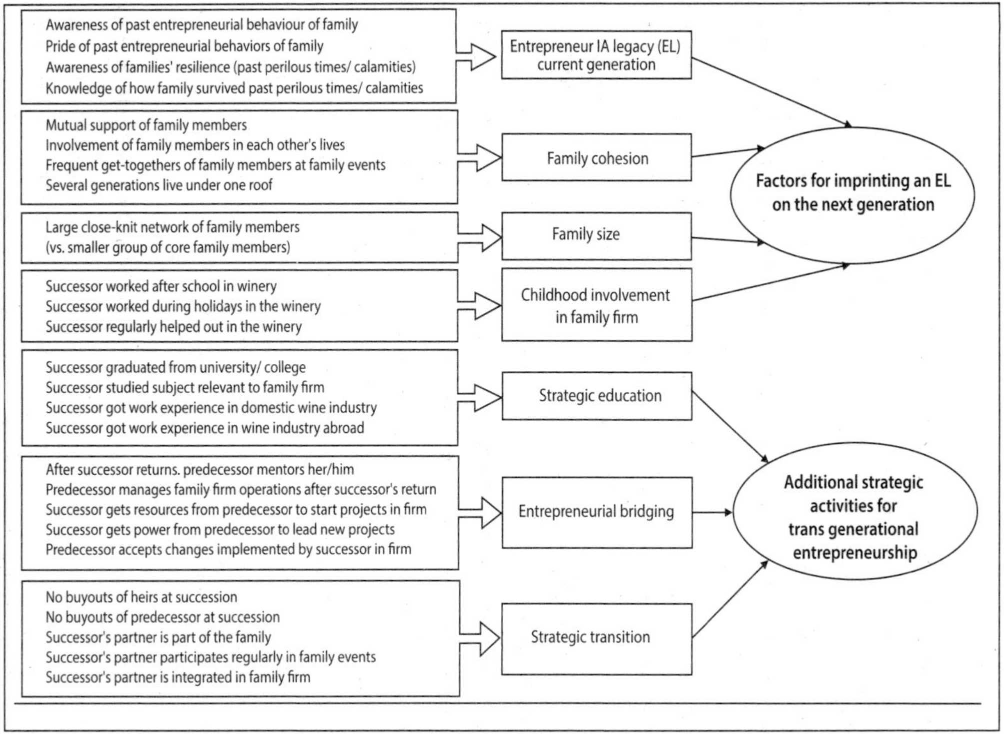

*Peter Jaskiewicz, James G. Combs and Sabine B. Rau, 'Entrepreneurial legacy: Toward a theory of how some family firms nurture transgenerational entrepreneurship'. *Journal of Business Venturing* 30(1) August 2014.

got the best firm), and a professional consultant is now mapping the competence profiles of all family members to see who should be on the board of which company. Managing the family, not family management, is the way of the future.[89]

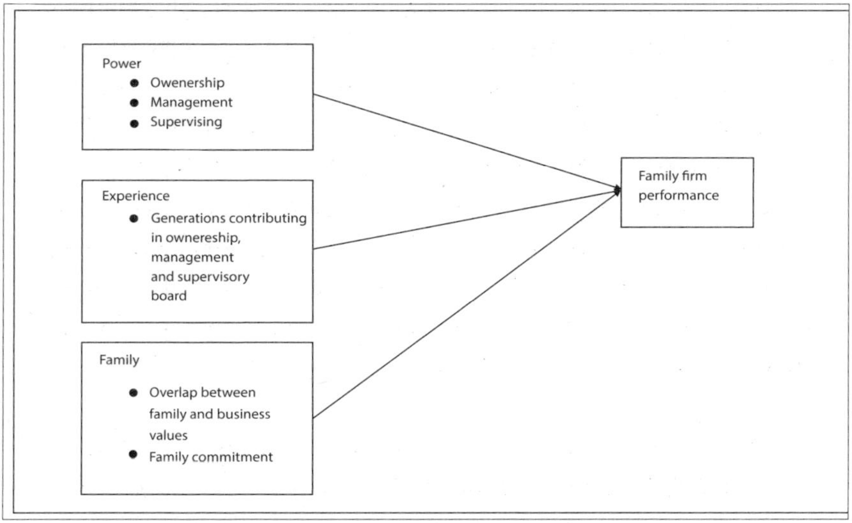

Figure 6.3 Family Firm Performance[90]

At LEGO Group, one of the world's leading toy manufacturers based in Denmark, now in its third generation, family members have consciously divided their activities among various parts of the business. The basis for this is a strong

[89]https://www.business-standard.com/article/companies/murugappa-group-to-drop-20-year-old-corp-advisory-board-as-part-of-revamp-120112400762_1.html

[90]Avendano-Alcaraz, Jorge, et al. 'A family-based competitive advantage: handling key success family factors in Mexican family businesses.' Cuadernos de Administración 22.39 (2009): pp. 191–212.

bond of understanding, respect and support and fostering one another's growth into new responsibilities.

In Ramesh Chandra's family, roles are defined according to each person's calibre and capability. He was the head of the family and the business. After his death, Sudhir now heads the group, Girish looks after sales and marketing while Pawan handles advertising. The family still lives together under one roof and has at least one meal in a day together, a tradition that has been followed since Ramesh Chandra's time because he believed that a 'family that eats together, stays together'. "We would have dinners together which would begin with casual conversations about everyday life, but inevitably, they would veer toward business matters. Work was his driving force," recalls Sudhir.

According to a Credit Suisse report, India has 108 publicly listed family owned businesses, third highest in the world, while China tops the tally with 167 such companies followed by the US which has 121. With an average market capitalisation of $6.5 billion, India ranks 5th in Asia Pacific excluding Japan, and 22nd globally, in terms of average m-cap. Besides China, the US and India, the top 10 countries in terms of number of family owned companies include France (4th place), Hong Kong (5th), Korea (6th), Malaysia (7th), Thailand (8th), Indonesia (9th), Mexico (10th). However, in terms of average size, the ranking changes much more in favour of developed markets, the report said. Average market capitalisation of family owned companies is greatest in Spain ($30 billion), the Netherlands ($30 billion), Japan ($24 billion) and Switzerland ($22 billion), the report that covered close to 1,000 family owned, publicly listed companies by region, sector and size said. It further said that Indian companies surveyed are more mature, with 60 per cent of family businesses in their third generation compared to 30 per cent of Chinese companies. The financial performance of family owned companies is also superior to that of non-family owned peers. Furthermore, family businesses appear to focus more on long-term growth and they have outperformed peers in terms of share price returns. At country-level, Chinese, Indian and Indonesian family owned companies appear to be the most expensive, trading at high absolute multiples, with a 12-month median price to earnings (P/E) of 15–16 times, compared to around 10–13 times P/E multiples of companies in Korea, Hong Kong and Singapore.[91]

Dainik Bhaskar practices GREAT values of *Ground Connect, Result Orientation, Emotional Connect, Analytical and Trend Setter*. This is imbibed by the people beginning from their induction into the company. Employees are recognised and awarded on the birthday of Ramesh

[91]https://www.credit-suisse.com/media/assets/corporate/docs/about-us/research/publications/the-cs-family-1000.pdf

Chandra on exhibiting these values in their work across the year. The selection is based on the evaluation by the peers and the superiors. "These values are evident even in the content. Ramesh Chandra was a stickler for creating content that readers would find personally relevant. It would be presented accordingly. The quality of content and production has been the key to our success, even when it required investing in higher technologies," says Shrawan Garg, who was brought as editor during the Jaipur launch.

7

Building Block by Block

August 1958, Bhopal. Birth of *Dainik Bhaskar*. Dwarka Prasad Agarwal, father of Ramesh Chandra Agarwal, was a man of resolute determination and had an astute sense of business acumen. He moved to Bhopal, Madhya Pradesh, from Jhansi, Uttar Pradesh, in the early 1950s and started a stationery business and later a publishing unit where he published notebooks for schools. It was here that the news bug bit him, and he simultaneously started publishing a Hindi newspaper, *Prakash*. He was unstoppable after he earned admiration and appreciation for his work. His first step was to rechristen *Prakash* to *Bhaskar* in 1958. Dwarka Prasad's *Bhaskar* expanded, and with it came an expansion of office and business. He set up several businesses, mainly paper mills, in Bhopal. Media's influence brought him close to people in power. He was always on good terms with political leaders in the states as well as in the Centre.

Like father, like son

Though completely different, Ramesh Chandra was his father's son. Business ran in his blood. Being inducted into the newspaper business very early in life helped him learn the ropes of the trade. He started in the dispatch department of *Dainik Bhaskar* where he would fold newspapers into bundles and take them to the market. He was a quick learner and picked up trade tricks very fast. Interactions with hawkers in the market taught him his first lesson of the trade – *market ko kya chahiye* (what does market want) and sell that to the market.

His soft demeanour belied the tough mettle he was built of. Failures usually take a toll on a person's morale, but defeats could never subdue Ramesh Chandra's optimism. Neither the two successive failures early in his career – both *Aftaab-e-Jadeed* in Urdu and *National Mail* in English could not take off – nor the one later in his life – the *DNA* debacle – could undermine his positive outlook. He would move on as there would always be another citadel waiting to be conquered.

In the conflict with and separation from his father, Ramesh Chandra scripted his success. It was a blockbuster script that gave *Dainik Bhaskar* a new avatar. From the launch of its first edition in 1983 in Indore, the newspaper has gone on to conquer citadels in different states, and today it is India's No.1 Hindi daily. In the previous chapters, we have seen how Ramesh Chandra established his brand and expanded his business beyond the newspaper. A keen observer, he would absorb and analyse market trends and take steps to set up new ventures, even beyond the realms of media. "He remained a learner all his life. When we wanted to enter Chandigarh, he spent a lot of time talking to people from all walks of life. The city was the administrative headquarter of two states. But it was a sleepy town. The main fodder for a newspaper, politics, crime and rallies, was not available. Based on the inputs from his interactions and our market research, we developed a new kind of newspaper that was centred on relevance and quality of content and production," states Pawan.

The ownership structure

Ramesh Chandra kept the structure of his organisation conservative but straight. He remained the founder-chairman till his last breath. He gave the reins of the newspaper business to his sons. This way he was able to focus more on diversification and expansion. It is important to periodically reanalyse a family business and see where it stands and how it is doing, especially during times of transition. The model that once worked well may not necessarily work for another generation. Rather than burdening family relationships, it is important to create a system that benefits everyone and supports business growth.

The simplest model is that of owner-operator, wherein ownership and control are with one person. It can be successful for more than one generation, for e.g., the East India Company. For this model to work, the family members' decision as to who would be the successor to the owner matters.[92]

Gaining control of *Dainik Bhaskar* was not easy for Ramesh Chandra. Though a dynamic man, his father was averse to any change that Ramesh Chandra wanted to introduce. Both stood their grounds. If father was more focused on the day's profits, son had his vision set on the future. Ramesh Chandra began working on the makeover of the daily because he wanted it to have a wider reach. So, out went treadle printing machine, Varityper and cylinder printer. Dainik Bhaskar got its first offset machine and new-age cameras for photo processing for the Bhopal edition. The year 1980 saw words being composed on computers. He was a patient man but was restless to improve the look of *Dainik Bhaskar*. He took one step at a time towards making it at par with English dailies. Once *Dainik Bhaskar* got a facelift, increasing its tally was not difficult, which till then was an uphill task because advertisers would turn their backs to him due to its poor quality. The next step was obvious – venture outside of Bhopal. He faced resistance from his father, but Ramesh Chandra had to take *Dainik Bhaskar* to a wider audience.

[92]'The 5 Models of Family Business Ownership' by Josh Baron and Rob Lachenauer, 20 September 2016, https://hbr.org/2016/09/the-5-models-of-family-business-ownership#:~:text=The%20breakthrough%20came%20only%20after,distributed%2C%20nested%2C%20and%20public.

Around the time India got independence, my grandfather sold home products and incense sticks in Mysore. The second generation grew the business on the foundation built by my grandfather. From a very young age, the second generation encouraged us, the third generation, to be a part of the business discussions. As a young boy I used to accompany my father to the market for sales and marketing of agarbattis. This exposure helped me understand the family, the business and most importantly, the distinction between the two. Today, my son accompanies me to office during his summer vacations. Our family also created a path to learn different parts of the business and created opportunities to work in different businesses. The second generation had one main business and my father and uncles were given to manage different verticals of the business within defined rules. When my cousins and I joined the business, the business had expanded beyond incense sticks and each one of us managed the chosen business independently. Moreover, regardless of the size of the business, the salary, allowances and perks available to each member is the same. *Arjun Ranga, Cycle Pure Agarbattis*[93]

Ramesh Chandra brought in his sons early in their lives. He knew getting them involved in the family business

[93]https://www.pwc.in/assets/pdfs/publications/2018/family-legacy-and-you.pdf.

later in their lives could prove hard because it's difficult to develop talents within the business and put them to good use. He had worked so hard to build his newspaper that it was important to plan their transition in such a way that they could find their own path in the world and then successfully boomerang back into their respective roles in the family business. Families tend to undertake actions such as:

Finding right roles. When planning for the next generation, owners often have their eyes set on one role, that of the CEO. Ramesh Chandra had different plans. Walking in his father's footsteps, he inducted his firstborn while he was in his teens. He believed it was important to start the process early because 'multiple roles that are essential to effective ownership cannot be outsourced'. After Ramesh Chandra's demise, Sudhir heads the business, Girish handles sales and marketing and Pawan is the technology person.

Getting the group dynamic right. It's important to guide the next-generation owners to work together and communicate. Ramesh Chandra had very open discussions with his sons because he understood that decisions made after consultation and discussion would boost his sons' confidence and prepare them to become smart decision-makers. He believed that they must have a say in all decisions as they were involved in the business. He had made it mandatory for the family to have at least one meal together.

They would talk on different subjects but eventually Ramesh Chandra would end up discussing business, which was always on his mind. Even today, the family continues with the practice. Festivals are celebrated together. They go on vacation along with all the members.

Finding a collective voice. Ramesh Chandra and his father were never on the same page. But he came into his own after he left his father's house. His sons saw a transformation in their father that they liked and were in awe of. He found his own voice after the split from his father. His sons found theirs under the guidance of their father. He showed them the power of a collective voice and made them see if they speak individually, their power as owners will diminish. "We have family board meeting every month. While business is at core, in this meeting we discuss how the family grows together as well as how we remain accountable to each other," says Pawan.

Perspective and expectations among the senior and next generations differ. Open and honest conversations can help bridge this gap. Most of the next generation feel that they performed better and learned more when they were given the room to make decisions and more importantly, make mistakes. Exposure to education and external work experience brings to the table ideas on modernisation, professionalism, bringing in external subject matter experts, digitalisation and innovation in the family business. The next generation feels that the senior generation should be more open to ideas and seek more delegation and decentralisation. The next generation acknowledge that to make inroads into their roles in the business, they have to demonstrate skills, exhibit patience, take the counsel of experienced business leaders – family or non-family – and take decisions on the basis of information, study, trials and preparation. The process is meticulous, but once there is a solid base of transparent communication between generations and constructive discussions around career paths, alignment of generational ambitions for the business becomes possible. Commitment to the business and willingness to invest time are critical for two generations to work together.[94]

Innovation and diversification: keys to surviving and thriving

Innovation is the key to sustaining family owned firms. Family members must realise that rewards are earned for the work they do and not because they are owners. Roles of each member should be clear to all. The founder of a family business enjoys certain values, and because of their

[94]'Family, Legacy and You', https://www.pwc.in/assets/pdfs/publications/2018/family-legacy-and-you.pdf.

position in the family and firm, they will 'exert considerable influence on the culture, values and performance of their firms during and beyond their tenure'.[95, 96]

It is also observed that the set of values that entrepreneurs rely on change with time. Values, such as ambition, reliability, responsibility, hard work, honesty, and growth[97] are found to be practiced more during the setting up of the business and other values of openness or the ability to consider other perspectives and values, are witnessed more during the organisation's long-term survival and growth.[98]

Businesses, especially small and medium-sized enterprises (SMEs), suffer if they do not change with the change in political, economic, social and technological scenarios. Managing change deftly is important to their survival and success because change is a reality that affects all.

Changes in the external environment can have a major influence on the ability of these firms to compete effectively. When new players enter the market, the longstanding competitiveness of SMEs that are unprepared for change can be undermined. Change management needs to be at

---

[95]García-Álvarez, Ercilia, and Jordi López-Sintas. 'A taxonomy of founders based on values: The root of family business heterogeneity.' Family Business Review 14.3 (2001): pp. 209–230.

[96]Sharma, P. 2004. An overview of the field of family business studies. Family Business Review, 17, pp. 1–36.

[97]Casson, M. (1992). 'Entrepreneurship: A model of risky innovation under capital constraints'. In G. Norman & M. La Manna (Eds.), *The new industrial economics* (pp. 186–213). Cheltenham: Edward Elgar.

[98]Bird, B. J. (1989). *Entrepreneurial behavior*. Glenview, Ill: Scott Foresman and Company.

the heart of the strategic management process. Managers need to understand the strategic framework within which the firm is operating. This includes a full understanding of the firm's existing strengths, weaknesses, opportunities and threats. Furthermore, the process includes identifying the change agent, be it internal of external to the industry.

Strategies adopted by family firms seem to have been designed keeping in mind financial security and control of the firm within the family unit, and different ways in which competitive market pressures influence the companies' strategic postures, depending on the stage in the company life cycle. How a firm redesigns its plan with evolving and changing internal capabilities and environmental conditions is a crucial outcome. In a closely held company, owner-managers usually design a plan at the founding of the organisation. It's their personal involvement that this commitment to the strategy often continues over time leading to unwillingness to change the original strategy.

At the Bhaskar Group, the sons have managed to keep the business flourishing because they still abide by the values and concerns instilled by their father. In his lifetime, the patriarch had handed over the newspaper business to the trio so that he could concentrate more on expansion and diversification of his brand. To grow, one must change and diversify with the times, he would say, because if one wants to follow growth one has to enter new verticals.

Inheriting a legacy brings several challenges; for successors, the most important challenge is the need to maintain their own identities as they extend the business. The shadow of the father looms large. The offices tend to have large photos of the founders reminding them about the value that they stood for and would need to be upheld with change in time. When Ratan Tata took charge after JRD, he inherited an empire but also the challenge of proving himself worthy of the responsibility as well as taking the group to newer heights. His efforts to bring Tata into passenger cars with Indica and Nano proved to be the clincher. He had proven as a great successor of JRD. Bringing Jaguar Land Rover into his fold added to his stature. His investments into online businesses made him a role model like any startup unicorn.

Success in diversification

There are examples when businesses chose to diversify and were successful. 'Xerox' was so synonymous with its core industry that it became common office parlance to ask for 'a Xerox' of a document, rather than a photocopy. It became a $10bn (€8.5bn) global company that is just as likely to offer consultation and training services as it is office technology. Similarly, the UK-based Virgin Group has successfully ventured into a host of different industries, from transport to entertainment.' When Swedish furniture firm IKEA entered the gig economy through its acquisition of the on-demand services platform TaskRabbit, it just extended its existing ecosystem.

Birla, Tata, Reliance, TVS, etc., are family firms that

have diversified to pursue growth and have become behemoths. The 109-year-old TVS Group recently decided to restructure its family holdings in the group companies. The restructuring has been done in a manner that will 'align and synchronise' the ownership of shares in various companies with the management of the respective businesses. The $8.5-billion group – started in 1911 by TV Sundaram Iyengar – is in diversified businesses including auto, auto component, logistics and finance (see chart), and over the years family members had invested in them either directly or through the holding companies (TV Sundram Iyengar & Sons Pvt Ltd, Sundaram Industries Pvt Ltd and Southern Roadways Pvt Ltd).[99]

> Post the family agreement, existing management of the various listed and unlisted businesses in the TVS Group will continue to be managed by the same family members. Thus, Suresh Krishna and his family will continue to manage Sundram Fasteners while Venu Srinivasan's family will run TVS Motor Company and Sundaram Clayton. Ram and his son Srivats Ram will manage Wheels India while S Viji and his son Sriram Viji will handle Brakes India. R Dinesh will continue to run the logistics and the after-market service businesses.[100]

[99]https://www.thehindubusinessline.com/companies/tvs-family-to-rejig-ownership-of-group-companies/article62187703.ece.

[100]https://economictimes.indiatimes.com/news/company/corporate-trends/will-members-of-the-fourth-generation-of-tvs-group-take-more-risks/articleshow/46913047.cms?from=mdr

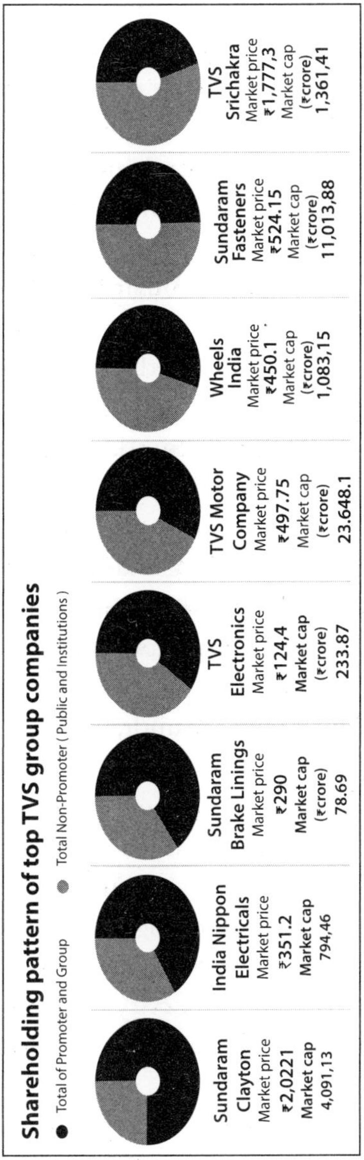

Source : Capital Line % holding as of September 2020 *as on December 10, 2020

Figure 7.1

If diversification is a way of building on existing success, it is also necessary for a firm's survival because of several factors like sudden change in consumer trends, new technologies storming the market and overhauling the entire scenario. Resilient are those that anticipate changes and adapt them before their core strength becomes outdated.

The Finnish firm Nokia began life in the 1860s as a paper manufacturer. Upon seeing the growth of various new technologies, the company eventually entered the telecoms space, becoming the world's best-selling mobile phone brand by the late 1990s. However, as the industry developed, Nokia was unable to shift its focus to software, eventually falling behind smartphone developers like Apple as a result. But Nokia was able to successfully diversify into unrelated industries throughout the 20th century, but the rapid growth of the app economy caught the company by surprise.[101]

Key to survival

Businesses face ups and downs. Some become obsolete with the emergence of new technologies and eventual shift in markets while others diversify to strengthen their core industry as well as branch out to expand its

[101]https://www.europeanceo.com/finance/why-diversifying-your-business-doesnt-always-bring-success/

growth. For many it's difficult to predict which industries will add value to their business and which will add to their problems. We have discussed in earlier chapters how the Bhaskar Group successfully launched several editions and ventured into different sectors. Except media and realty, the group has not been able to sustainably develop other businesses like textiles, oil and cement. Experts say one of the main reasons businesses fail in their diversification efforts is because their plan is not in the right place. There must be a careful thought process behind any strategy – whether there are enough resources or capabilities that can be channelised as per market demands to stay ahead of competition. However, simply having adequate money to start something new is not always enough because money is not the only resource that dictates market behaviour.

Ramesh Chandra was ambitious and restless; he kept seeking growth outside his territory, i.e., media. He invested in liquor business when somebody suggested there was a lot of money involved, but shut it down after a few months as it went against his morale. He then tried his hands at oil, cement and textiles but couldn't succeed. Notably, these were unrelated industries in which he was seeking to diversify and become an industrialist. Though an experienced and successful media baron, he understood he lacked the knowledge and resources needed to manage business activities in unrelated sectors. "The Mumbai entry through *DNA* was a very big lesson for us. We learnt how one gets overwhelmed by markets, people and competitors. In the process, we lose our own DNA," recalls Girish. Entry into Mumbai was challenging as *Dainik Bhaskar* was getting into a metro city with an English paper where Hindi was not the main language of the population. The team adopted the same methodology of research, house-to-house access, winning distributors and building a product ground up. "There may be several factors leading to the failure. However, in my opinion, the most crucial was that we missed our core of finding fresh talent and giving them the lead. We hired a very experienced team from other media houses and without realising it, we had become like the other newspaper," adds Girish.

When to bring in independent non-family members

According to PwC India Family Business Survey, 2016, 81 per cent of respondents have non-family members on their board, higher than the global average of 65 per cent. Initially, many begin by having informal interactions with non-family members to get advice or suggestion on any idea or matter. Gradually, they are brought on board as independent directors. Non-family members bring in an external dimension, a wider perspective and provide an independent, unbiased view. It is important that non-family members on the board challenge family members, moderate and steer discussions and bring in a certain level of governance. They can also be a source of learning to the next generation and act as mentors.

The Bhaskar Group took early step towards bringing someone from outside the family as the CEO of My FM. Unlike other verticals that are headed by family members, this is headed by a non-family member. The team was selected from the group. The owners realised that there was a need to have the right people with the required skill sets at the helm who aligned with the company's values. It's important for the owners to have the ability to articulate their vision and ensure that the people are aligned with their vision and work culture.

Picking someone to head the realty vertical, DB Infrastructure Pvt. Ltd., was not as difficult as Ramesh Chandra had thought it to be. Ravi Datt Sawla, then in the accounts department of the group, proved to be a man with a mission and the vertical under him grew at an exponential rate. He successfully launched projects in Madhya Pradesh and its neighbouring states, and also revived a few dormant ones.

The Tata Group is a very complex organisation, owning many different companies but the ownership structure is highly difficult to grasp, seeing as there is cross-ownership and ambiguity regarding who makes the decisions, as per The Economist report. According to The Economist, Tata Sons mostly hold the decision rights as they have big influences regarding subsidiary board members, and the control of the Tata brand name. The Economist also suggests that Ratan Tata held a lot of power of the governance of both the Tata Trusts, Tata Sons, and individual Tata companies.

The companies are all bound together by Tata Sons, which, in turn, is controlled by the Tata trusts, holding close to 66%, with power lying with the Tata family. As a side note, the largest non-Tata stockholder is the Shapoorji Pallonji Group, which controls 18.4% of Tata Sons. While each publicly traded company in the group is an independent entity, with a CEO and a board of directors (with a fiduciary responsibility to protect the shareholders of that company), the independence is illusory. Not only does Tata Sons own a significant piece of each company, all the companies own shares in each other (cross holdings effectively controlled by the family group) and directors representing family group interests serve on each board. Though much is made of the conglomerate nature of the Tata Group, the group derives the bulk of its value (>70%) from TCS, a technology company that derives most of its revenues from outside India. It is a testimonial to the stability and continuity in the Tata Group that it has had only six men at its helm over its 150-year history.[102]

[102]https://www.livemint.com/Companies/ag69hpmUl4PjDbQoe3tvvK/Chandras-true-test-will-be-shutting-down-Tatas-lossmaking.html.

When to take a back seat

Ramesh Chandra had been successful in most of the businesses. The group had been on a roller-coaster ride setting new vistas. Dainik Bhaskar had become a conglomerate. Media was still the largest business, but real estate, power, textile and oil extraction were equally significant. However, the period between 2010 and 2015 was different. Several of the businesses were not yielding the desired results. New ventures were not so successful. Ramesh Chandra felt that there was a need to relook at the way he had grown so far. 'I believe we need to rethink the way we are managing our growth. The market forces are behaving differently. It may be prudent to focus on consolidation than diversification,' said Ramesh Chandra to his sons during a breakfast meeting. 'Seems that I also need a cooling and refresher break. There is need for a rethink and to rationalise our portfolio. Please develop a plan accordingly,' he added.

"From that day onwards for the next three years he stopped participating actively. He was available to us when needed but would not ask about the business. He would attend the board meetings more as a protocol," says Girish. But Ramesh Chandra would not stop working. He diverted his focus to social causes. He enhanced his involvement with social and religious groups. In the meantime, the group exited some of the businesses and consolidated the media business and strongly developed digitally. In 2015, when he noticed that growth in the newspaper had stagnated, he came back to play an active role to provide new ways to grow. He remained active till his last days with the same energy.[103]

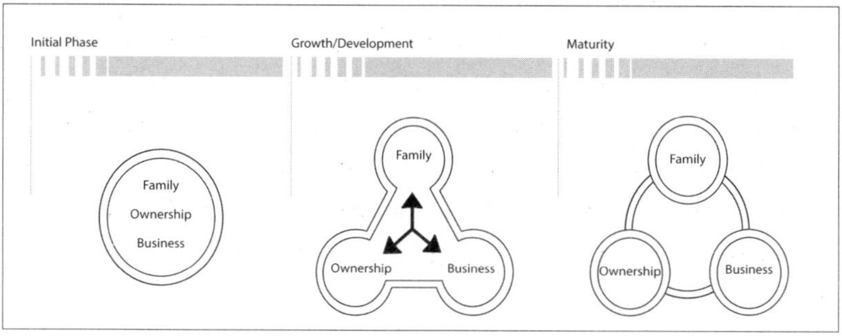

According to a McKinsey research, 'to be successful as both the company and the family grow, a family business must meet two intertwined challenges: achieving strong business performance and keeping the family committed to and capable of carrying on as the owner. Five dimensions of activity must work well and in synchrony: harmonious relations within the family and an understanding of how it should be involved with the business, an ownership structure that provides sufficient capital for growth while allowing the family to control key parts of the business, strong governance of the company and a dynamic business portfolio, professional management of the family's wealth, and charitable foundations to promote family values across generations'.[104]

[103]https://www.oecd.org/daf/ca/corporategovernanceprinciples/43654301.pdf
[104]'The Five Attributes of Enduring Family Businesses'by Christian Caspar, Ana Karina Dias, and Heinz-Peter Elstrodt, McKinsey.com, January 1, 2010,

"His legacy lives on through several businesses as well as the many social activities that the group keeps engaged in. Ramesh Chandra would say *growth hai to business hai; growth hai to family hai*," remembers Pawan.

---

https://www.mckinsey.com/business-functions/people-and-organisational-performance/our-insights/the-five-attributes-of-enduring-family-businesses.